Money Back Guarantee!

Your money back if The Greedy Home Buyer's Guide doesn't save you any money!*

If you're planning on buying a house in Washington or Oregon, you absolutely must have this book!

The Greedy Home Buyer's Guide will save you thousands! Learn how to negotiate with real estate agents, sellers, lenders, closing agents, and countless others.

Dealing with agents —
- ✓ The four things to look for in a real estate agent
- ✓ What agents don't want you to know

Which house to buy —
- ✓ Picking a house that makes the best investment for future appreciation

Getting a loan —
- ✓ Which loan program will save you the most
- ✓ Improving your loan profile to get the best rate
- ✓ Insider secrets of the mortgage industry

Negotiating —
- ✓ 19 winning negotiation tactics

Contracts —
- ✓ Tests to determine if a contract is enforceable
- ✓ Using contingencies to your advantage

Dan Lumley has been teaching real estate at the college level since 1977. While teaching real estate has always been close to his heart, Dan has also kept himself actively involved in the real world of residential real estate sales and financing in the northwest. Dan's students know him as an expert in all aspects of real estate.

For many years Dan has held his popular seminars for home buyers. His experience teaching first-time buyers and his extensive knowledge of real world real estate combine to make this the most readable and authoritative book on buying a home in the Pacific northwest.

There are lots of books for first-time buyers. There is only one that promises to save you money!

* Money back guarantee: If you read this book and it doesn't save you money, return it with your sales receipt to Real Estate Publishers, Inc., 8316 N. Lombard, #329, Portland, Oregon 97203 for a full refund. *Do not return to place of purchase.* Please allow two weeks for refund.

Pacific Northwest Edition

THE GREEDY HOME BUYER'S GUIDE

Dan Lumley, Realtor

Library of Congress Cataloging in Publication Data:
Lumley, Dan, Realtor
    The Greedy Home Buyer's Guide
    ISBN 1-878572-11-3
    1. House Buying — United States. 1. Title
    Library of Congress Card Number 00-105749

Copyright 2000, Real Estate Publishers, Inc. All rights reserved. Except as provided in Sections 107 or 108 of the United States Copyright Act of 1976 and amendments thereto, no part of this publication may be reproduced in any form or by any means, or stored in any electronic system without prior written permission of Real Estate Publishers, Inc.

ISBN 1-878572-11-3

This book contains the opinions and ideas of its author. It is designed to provide accurate and authoritative information regarding the purchase of real estate. It is sold with the understanding that neither the author nor the publisher is rendering tax, accounting, legal or other professional services. If tax, accounting, legal or other expert advice is required, the reader should seek the services of a qualified professional. Any references to organizations, forms, products, trademarks, or service marks do not imply an endorsement or recommendation.

Set in Monotype Garamond
Printed in the United States of America
First printing, July, 2000

Real Estate Publishers, Inc.
8316 N. Lombard #329
Portland, Oregon 97203-3727

Quantity discounts are available for use as premiums and sales promotions. Contact publisher for information.

Contents

Chapter 1 **To Buy or Not to Buy, That Is the Question** 9
- Why over 70% of northwesterners own their own home, and why most of the rest should rent
- Income tax laws that favor homeowners
- Live in a house for free! Really!
- How to get a 200% annual rate of return on the investment in your home

Chapter 2 **Gypsies, Tramps and Thieves** 19
- Different kinds of real estate agents
- Legal issues you *must* know when dealing with agents
- Why you need a buyer's agent
- Secrets about commissions that agents don't want you to know
- Traps in exclusive buyer agency agreements and how to avoid them
- What to look for in an agent and how to find a good one
- How to buy properties that are not listed and still be represented by a buyer's agent

Chapter 3 **You'll Appreciate Appreciation** 49
- What makes real estate go up in value
- Which goes up faster, single-family detached house, condominium, manufactured dwelling, or small plex?
- Old or new, which gives the greatest appreciation?
- Advantages and disadvantages of the fixer-upper
- Leave the dogs for others — spotting the losers
- How important is location, really? Statistics disprove an old real estate adage
- Are there profits in distressed properties?

Chapter 4 **The Art of the Deal** 67
- Negotiating starts by becoming an expert about property values
- Comparative market analysis and appraisal, two different approaches
- Distressed properties — can you get a house for ten cents on the dollar?
- He who cares least, wins!
- Pitching and closing, controlling the scene
- Nineteen top negotiation strategies guaranteed to save you thousands!

Chapter 5 **Have I Got a Program for You!** 87
- How lenders work
- Why the secondary market calls the tune
- Types of primary lenders and what some of them hope you don't know
- Can you save money with a discount or buydown?
- Federal Housing Administration
- Federal Department of Veterans Affairs
- Zero down payment programs
- Using state programs to get a loan at below market interest rate and low down payment
- Zero down payment and low interest rate options for rural housing
- Conventional loans — fixed, adjustable, hybrid, combination — and how to determine which is best
- When it's a good idea to assume a loan and when it's a mistake
- Seller financing and how to negotiate the terms you want

Chapter 6 **Honest, I Can Handle the Payments!** 123
- Prequalification or preapproval, which do you need?
- Your credit report and how to patch it up
- Credit scoring — the infamous FICO score and how to enhance yours

- How to manipulate qualifying ratios in your favor
- Why you must pay for an appraisal and how appraisers work

Chapter 7 Beware the Predatory Lender! 135
- Detecting a predatory lender
- Armament and weapons of defense

Chapter 8 The Large Print Giveth and the Fine Print Taketh Away 143
- Basic requirements of contract law, when a contract is not enforceable
- How to make an offer
- Using counteroffers effectively
- Contract problems — fraud and misrepresentation
- Why professionals always use contingencies
- Understanding earnest money agreement forms and their common provisions
- But the sellers removed the light fixtures! Knowing what is supposed to be included
- Why options and lease options are probably not in your best interests

Chapter 9 An Escrow is Not a Large Noisy Bird 167
- Why can't I just trade them the money for the keys? Understanding the function of the closing agent
- Walking through the closing process
- The closing instructions and how to make sure they are correct
- The Real Estate Settlement Procedures Act protects you only if you understand how to use it
- Closing expenses and who is to pay them
- Common mistakes closing agents make and how to check for them

Appendix A 187
Seller Property Disclosure Forms

Appendix B 205
   Amortization Chart and How to Use a Financial Calculator

Resources 209
   Names and Addresses of Organizations

Index 217

Chapter 1

To Buy or Not to Buy, That Is the Question

OK, that isn't exactly what Shakespeare said, but then in Shakespeare's day becoming a homeowner was a lot simpler matter. If Shakespeare were trying to buy a home today he would probably have written a soliloquy about it too.

If this is your second home, then you already know you want to be a homeowner. The rest of you bought this book because you're considering the idea and need to finalize the decision. Either way, you can't do the job right without starting with some idea of why you are buying a home.

First things first. Start by making yourself a list of what you want in a home. What do you want your home to do for you? Why are you buying? Arrange your goals in order by priority. Every buyer has various reasons for buying, for example —

- Independence from the landlord
- Appreciation
- Build up equity instead of a collection of rent receipts
- Pride, project image of success to others
- Room for special interests and hobbies
- A place for kids or pets

You won't be happy in your new home unless you are honest here. Be brutal with yourself. Better to have a clear understanding of why you are doing this right up front. And include your partner. Relationships are hard enough without working at cross purposes with each other.

Once you have your goals firmly in mind and prioritized,

you can translate them into specific needs. If pride is your highest priority, then a fancy neighborhood should be at the top of your list of wants, even if it means all you can afford is a tiny house. If the kids are your top priority, then enough bedrooms and a neighborhood with top quality schools should top your list. See how this allows you to create a prioritized shopping list? We can't always get everything we want, but this way you can be more sure of getting those things that are most important to you.

Now, don't get all panicky and assume you need to go into psychotherapy to be sure you have all your deep-down motivations figured out. This is not the last house you are going to buy. Just do the best you can. If your list of priorities isn't perfect, it won't be fatal. Believe me. I've made lots of mistakes buying homes, and I'm still here to talk about it.

Once you have an idea what kind of home you are looking for, you need to look at the financial aspect. Later, we'll investigate financing options and what you can qualify for, but for now, you need to decide if buying a home makes financial sense in the first place.

If you are a first-time buyer, presumably you are currently renting. The question is, is it more financially advantageous to buy, or to continue as a renter? For the moment, never mind about the emotional satisfaction of being a homeowner, let's just look at the financial aspects separately for a moment.

If you've never owned a home before you're probably unfamiliar with the costs and financial benefits of home ownership. You know there will be mortgage payments, but have you considered what is included in those payments — as compared to your rent payment? And as for your rent payment, do you know what operating costs your landlord covers with it?

Let's look at your rent payment first. Most tenants blithely assume the landlord just puts their rent money in his or her pocket and gets richer and richer. Being a landlord myself, allow me to correct that misperception of reality. The landlord has bills to pay just like everyone else, including lots of bills to pay for the property. For example, your current apartment building or rental house is subject to property taxes. While many renters are happily ignorant of property taxes, rest assured, your landlord is not. They have to be paid. Guess where your landlord is getting the money to pay them?

Not only that, but the building must be covered by fire and casualty insurance. Guess where that money is coming from? You probably guessed both these right — your landlord pays the tax bill and the insurance premium out of your rent check. The point is that, when you buy a home you will have to make mortgage payments, and you will have to pay the taxes and insurance yourself as well.

Property taxes are a lien on the property which are ahead of your lender's mortgage, so your lender will want to be sure that you pay the taxes on time. If you didn't the county could foreclose on the property, which would extinguish the bank's mortgage. For some reason, bankers take a really dim view of this. Similarly, if the house burns down, your lender would be in bad shape if it weren't insured.

To make sure the taxes and insurance are paid, almost all mortgage loans are arranged so that your monthly mortgage payment includes an amount equal to the principal and interest payment, plus one-twelfth the annual taxes and one-twelfth the annual insurance premium. The result is that your monthly house payment is at least partially comparable to your monthly rent payment — your rent payment includes taxes and insurance, and so will your future mortgage payment.

However, there are additional costs of home ownership that are not the same as when renting. The number one such expense is maintenance. When you are renting and the plumbing springs a leak, you just pick up the phone. Ok, that doesn't always work as smoothly as it is supposed to, but at least you don't have to pay the plumber. Rest assured, though, if you are a homeowner, the plumber will send the bill to you, not your old landlord.

In addition to maintenance there are expenses of home improvements. Houses tend to soak up an amazing amount of money. Should you plant flowers in the springtime? Wouldn't a built-in bookcase look nice? These aren't maintenance, strictly speaking, but they sure aren't free either. You may consider these as additional investments in the property to be recovered when you sell, but not all improvements increase the value in proportion to the cost. And even if they do, you have to pay for them out of pocket when you make the improvements.

Before I scare you away from the idea of owning a home completely, on the plus side, there are also financial benefits of home ownership that renters do not gain. One of them is the deductibility of mortgage interest from your income tax. If you buy a home with a mortgage of $100,000 at 8% interest over 30 years, your principal and interest payments over the first year come to $8,805.12 ($733.76 per month). Of this, $7,969.82 is interest. You can see this in the following chart showing the amortization for the first twelve months of the loan —

Mo.	Beg. Bal.	Payment	Interest	Principal	New Balance
1	$100,000.00	733.76	666.67	67.10	99,932.90
2	99,932.90	733.76	666.22	67.55	99,865.36
3	99,865.36	733.76	665.77	68.00	99,797.36
4	99,797.36	733.76	665.32	68.45	99,728.91
5	99,728.91	733.76	664.86	68.91	99,660.01
6	99,660.01	733.76	664.40	69.36	99,590.64
7	99,590.64	733.76	663.94	69.83	99,520.82
8	99,520.82	733.76	663.47	70.29	99,450.52
9	99,450.52	733.76	663.00	70.76	99,379.76
10	99,379.76	733.76	662.53	71.23	99,308.53
11	99,308.53	733.76	662.06	71.71	99,236.82
12	99,236.82	733.76	661.58	72.19	99,164.62
	Totals	$8,805.12	$7,969.82	$835.38	

The neat thing for homeowners is that the $7,969.82 you pay in interest is deductible on your income tax as an itemized deduction. If you are in the 15% federal tax bracket, this means an annual tax savings of $1,195.47, or almost $100 a month. Oregon residents can add another 9% to the 15% figure, since most of them are paying that in state income tax. Either way, it's kind of nice, isn't it?

Not only that, due to intense lobbying by homebuilders and real estate agents, your annual property tax bill is also an itemized deduction. A modest home in the northwest runs an annual tax bill in the neighborhood of $1,500, so at a federal tax rate of 15%, add another $225 annual tax savings, or almost $20 a month. Renters don't get either of these benefits. All a renter gets is a shoebox full of rent receipts and canceled checks. Is home ownership sounding better?

I should interject here that the deductions for mortgage interest and property taxes are itemized deductions. These two deductions replace the standard deduction that all taxpayers are entitled to. In other words, the additional tax benefit to you will be less than the $100 and $20 mentioned above. How much less depends on how many other itemized deductions you have — charitable contributions, unreimbursed health costs, etc.

Then, of course, principal gain on the loan is another big benefit. From the chart above you can see that your ending balance on the $100,000 loan was only $99,164.62 at the end of the first year — a gain of $835.38. You sure don't see any of that as a renter. That adds another $70 or so a month that the renter doesn't get. And the longer you own the house, the faster the principal gain — look at the chart to see how the amount of principal gain goes up each month.

And if that isn't enough, add the potential for appreciation. Homes throughout the northwest have increased in market value at an average rate of approximately 8% per annum over the past 20 years.[1] If you paid $125,000 for the house, add another $10,000 a year, or about $833 a month that you don't see if you're a renter.

Let's see how the monthly financial benefits add up so far. Allowing, say one-half of the income tax savings (because they are itemized deductions and replace the standard deduction that you are already entitled to) we find the following might be typical —

---

[1] Statistics for Oregon and Washington from the Office of Federal Housing Enterprise Oversight. For the period from 12/31/94 to 12/31/99 average annual appreciation for Oregon was 6.64% and for Washington, 5.62%. For the 20-year period from 12/31/79 to 12/31/99 the average annual percentage increases were 7.67% for Oregon and 8.42% for Washington.

Income tax savings
    Interest deduction (half of $100) $50
    Property tax deduction (half of $20)   10
Principal gain   70
Appreciation   833
Total $963

Hmmm. How much did you say you were paying in rent right now? Can you afford *not* to buy a house?

Now, the above looks really good. It looks as though living in a house you own is practically free compared to renting. Well, it is, but there are some other considerations.

First, you have to make the mortgage payments, including principal, interest, one-twelfth the taxes and one-twelfth the insurance each month. For the usual starter home, this will be in the neighborhood of $1,000 a month. If you are a typical first-time buyer, this is probably a little more than you are paying in rent. You will get $963 of that back (according to the above figures), but not each month. You will get $130 per month back when you file your taxes each year, and the remaining $833 per month you will get back when you sell the home. In the meantime, the $1,000 monthly expense is cash out of pocket.

But there is yet another cool tax angle to home ownership. Most first-time homebuyers are young — young enough that they have probably never had to deal with the evils of capital gains taxes. Simply put, a capital gain happens when you sell something for more than you paid for it. The IRS has a nasty way of calling that income, and expecting their share of it. What if you bought a house for $125,000 today and sold it some years later for $250,000? That would be $125,000 of capital gain. Adding $125,000 to your regular income all in one year would put you in a very ugly tax bracket. The IRS would take a very large bite of that.

Well, luckily that won't happen, at least under current tax law. If you sold a rental house under that scenario you would pay the capital gains tax. Ditto if you made a capital gain on the sale of stocks, bonds, or any other asset. But if it is a personal residence, you are exempt from capital gains tax up to $250,000 of gain ($500,000 if married filing jointly). And you can do it every

Chapter 1, To Buy or Not to Buy, That Is the Question   15

two years if you keep buying new personal residences that often. Let me clarify what this means. It means tax-free income when you sell the personal residence. *Tax-free income!*

I mentioned that you can qualify for tax-free capital gains treatment every two years. While that is true, don't plan on buying and selling every couple of years. It costs about 7% of the sales price in sales expenses every time you sell. The 8% average annual increase in valuation we used in the calculations above is going to come to little or nothing if you sell only one year after you buy. Most people will tell you that it is not cost effective to buy at all unless you are going to live in the house for a minimum of two years. And even longer is a better idea. The longer you wait, the more you profit.

The chart below will give you an idea of what will happen to the value of a house purchased for $125,000 today, assuming the 8% annual value increase continues —

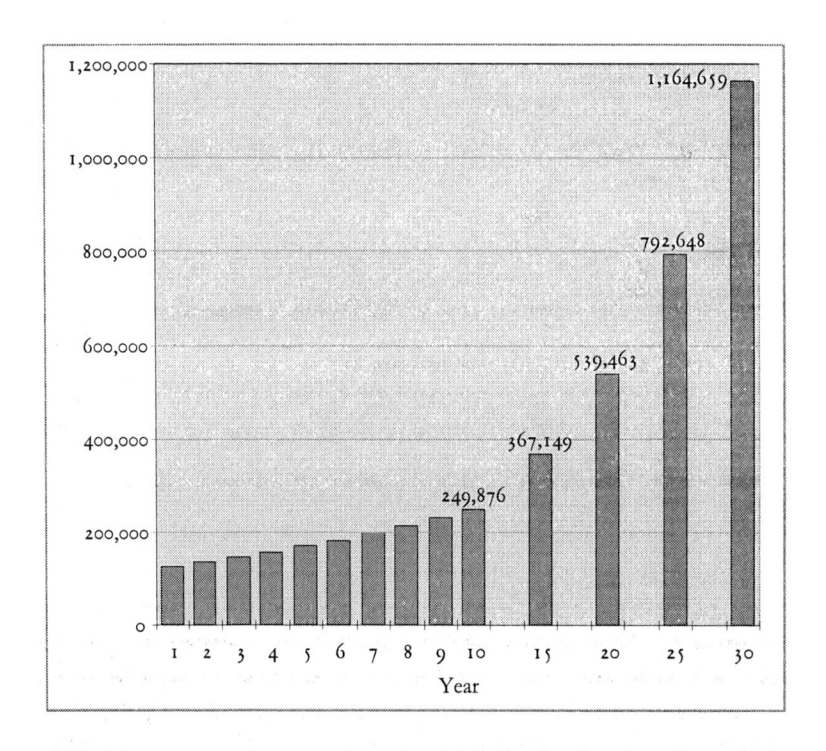

Year	Value
15	367,149
20	539,463
25	792,648
30	1,164,659

Additional chart values: Year 9 = 249,876

Pretty astonishing, isn't it? By the time you pay off the mortgage your house would be worth $1,164,659 — you'll be a millionaire! And before you pooh-pooh the idea, ask anyone who has owned a house for the past 10 years or more how much they paid for it. Be prepared for a shock.

While the chart shows the value of the house will go up dramatically, your monthly payment will go up only slightly. If you have a fixed rate mortgage, the principal and interest won't go up at all. And even if you have an adjustable rate mortgage, the increase can't be more than a couple hundred dollars because adjustable rate mortgages have a lifetime interest rate cap. And that is a worst-case scenario that will happen only if interest rates really skyrocket. For most homeowners, the only increase in their monthly payment will be due to annual increases in the property tax bill and insurance premiums.

If you think the potential for increasing monthly payments is a drawback to buying a home, consider what will happen if you continue to rent. Will your rent payment double in the next ten years? If you buy a house, even with an adjustable rate mortgage, I can virtually guarantee you that your monthly payment will not increase even half that much. Every homeowner knows that their monthly payments do not increase nearly as fast as their monthly housing expense would if they were still renters.

By now you may be getting a little confused with all this. Cheer up! There is an easier way to do it. Most real estate agents have software available that is programmed to answer the rent vs. buy question. You enter your tax rates, your current rent, the price range you are thinking of buying, answer a few other questions, and the software does the calculations for you. It still can't resolve the non-financial aspects (pride of ownership, space for your kids, etc.), but it does a good job showing you the financial pluses and minuses.

Buy now or wait?

When working with first-time buyers I find they frequently wonder if they might be better off waiting until they have a bigger down payment saved up. If you look at the amortization chart above, you can't help but be struck by the fact that the borrower pays $8,805.12 in payments the first year, but gets only $835.35 in principal gain. Having a bigger down payment certainly cuts down the astronomical amount of interest you will pay.

But waiting is almost always a mistake. Look at what the house is going to cost you every year you wait. If prices in the northwest keep going up at an average annual rate of 8%, then a $125,000 house today will cost $135,000 next year. You would have to be able to increase your savings account by $10,000 a year just to stay even.

But what if grandma's trust account is going to pay you a big chunk of cash in a couple of years? Would that make it more sensible to wait? The answer is still no. Even if the money you will receive is enough so you can pay cash for the house, you'd still be better off buying today. The reason is just arithmetic. If you buy today, you lock in today's price of the house. The interest you pay on the loan each year is less than the amount the house would go up in price if you wait. You either pay interest, or you pay a higher price. At today's appreciation rates, the interest is the cheaper of the two.

Leverage

Now, before moving on, I have to point out something that is probably going to shock you. Your home is a far better financial investment than the above figures make it look. Not that living in a place for free is not a good deal, but — even better — you will actually make a profit on it.

You see, your rate of return on an investment in a home is really an astronomical percentage. This is because your investment is not the purchase price, but rather, just the down payment. Suppose your mortgage was, indeed, $100,000, and the purchase price was $125,000, as in the above example. That means you made a down payment of $25,000. (Yeah, I know that is unrealistic for most people, but bear with me here for a minute.)

Now look at the amount of appreciation. Remember the dollar amount of appreciation in the northwest (from the above figures) is $10,000 every year (8% of the $125,000 purchase price).

But your cash investment is just $25,000 — the down payment — your investment is not the whole purchase price. On an investment of $25,000, an annual return of $10,000 is a rate of 40%. Show me a bank savings account that pays 40% interest. Show me any investment with the stability and safety of real estate that pays a 40% annual return.

Now consider what would happen if your down payment was a more realistic $5,000 instead of $25,000. A return of $10,000 a year on an investment of $5,000 is a 200% rate of return! Are you beginning to see why over 70% of the people in the northwest are homeowners?

Buying a property with a low down payment and then reaping the return based on the entire purchase price is called "leverage." It is a principle well known to real estate investors. Fortunes have been made using leverage. There is no reason you can't share in the benefits of leverage too. If you want to use leverage to maximize your rate of return, the principle is very simple — the less cash out of pocket, the higher the percentage of return. That means you just need to keep the down payment and closing costs low. Appreciation in the marketplace will take care of the rest.

If all the above sounds good, then you're getting close to going house hunting, but first you need to get a real estate agent. For more detail on that, see the next chapter on dealing with agents.

When you have to make a choice and don't make it, that in itself is a choice.
MARK TWAIN

Chapter 2

Gypsies, Tramps and Thieves

In truth, of all the people you will run into in your home buying adventure, real estate agents are probably the most honorable. Probably this is because they have been so highly regulated for so long. Still, you're going to have major problems and potentially lose a fortune if you don't know how they operate. In the past, this was pretty simple, but today it has become far more complex.

Unfortunately, understanding the rules is kind of academic and boring. Whatever you do, do not skip this chapter because it seems tedious. If you do, it could cost you thousands. So grit your teeth and plow through what I'm about to tell you.

Before we plunge into this issue, some terminology is important. I'm sure you've heard the terms "agent," "broker," "Realtor®," "sales associate," "salesperson," and perhaps even "associate broker." All of these people represent buyers and sellers, but the terms have different meanings.

Let's start with the licensing issues. The first license a real estate agent gets is called a "salespersons" license. "Sales associate" is a synonym for salesperson. A *salesperson* can work only under a broker. Think of it as a bit like an apprenticeship, although many very successful agents never bother to obtain any higher license. While licensed under a broker, a salesperson may conduct pretty much any real estate activity, except run a company independently. A *broker*, in contrast, can run his or her own company and hire salespersons as employees. It takes additional education and experience, plus an additional examination to become a broker.

An *associate broker* is someone who has met all the requirements of a broker, but chooses to work for another broker instead of running a business independently. Think of an associate broker as someone who could be independent, but chooses to continue working as a salesperson. Salespersons, brokers and associate brokers can all be referred to as "licensees."

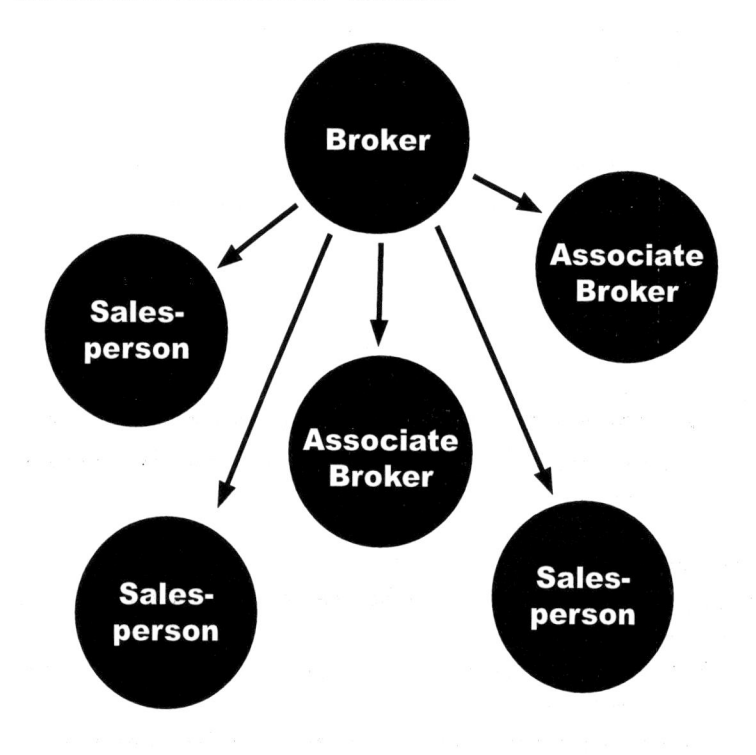

```
                    Broker
         ↙        ↙   ↓   ↘
   Sales-                    Associate
   person                     Broker
         ↘        ↓        ↙
              Associate
               Broker
         ↙                    ↘
   Sales-                      Sales-
   person                      person
```

A Realtor® is someone who belongs to the National Association of Realtors® (NAR) and agrees to abide by their code of ethics. The NAR coined the term "Realtor®" and registered it as a service mark, which is why it is supposed to be capitalized and have the little "®" symbol after it. Don't worry about the details of punctuation here; even Realtors® sometimes don't do it right. The important thing is that a Realtor® could be a broker, an associate broker, or a salesperson, because any licensee can join the NAR. All it means is that if someone is a Realtor®, then you know they consider real estate a profession and have agreed to standards of ethics beyond just what the state licensing laws demand.

The majority of licensees are members of NAR but you may

run into some who are not. You can tell if an agent is a member because non-members are not permitted to use the term "Realtor®," while members almost always state it on their business cards and in advertising.

Agents who are Realtors® may also have some additional letters after their names. One to look for is "CRS," which stands for "Certified Residential Specialist." Another is "GRI," which means "Graduate of the Realtor® Institute. A third is "CRB," which is a Certified Residential Broker. It takes several years of experience and additional education to earn these designations, so you know you are dealing with someone knowledgeable and professional. This is not to say that an agent without designations may not be the best agent for you. All other things being equal, I'd rather have an agent who has several years of experience than one with lots of letters after his or her name.

The law of agency

Now that we have the basic terminology out of the way, we need to get into the law of agency. An *agent* is someone who works for another, called a *principal*. If a licensee is working for you, then you are the principal and the licensee is the agent. Think of an agent as an employee, at least in one sense of the word. But unlike an ordinary employee, an agent owes fiduciary duties to the principal. These duties include loyalty, obedience, confidentiality, due diligence, full disclosure and fair dealings. For example, if the agent is representing a buyer the agent must disclose —

• The fair market value of the property (although the agent is not required to be a licensed appraiser),

• Any relationship the agent has with third parties (e.g., if the agent is representing you, but is related to the seller),

• Any facts the agent knows about the other side (e.g., if your agent knows why the seller is selling),

• Any offers or counteroffers as soon as received (usually considered to be "as soon as practicable"),

• The legal provisions of any offer (although a real estate agent is not allowed to give legal advice).

These duties are never absolute — for example, the duty of

full disclosure generally means only facts pertinent to the agency. Nevertheless, when you are shopping for a house, do you want the real estate agent to owe the duties of loyalty, obedience, confidentiality, due diligence and full disclosure to you? Or to the seller? Kind of important, isn't it?

Who is your agent?

Next we'll look at who represents whom. There are three possibilities. The agent can represent the seller (seller agency), the agent can represent the buyer (buyer agency), or the agent can represent both (dual agency). Seller agency and buyer agency are sometimes referred to as "single agencies," to distinguish them from dual agency.

When sellers list a property, the listing is probably taken by a salesperson or associate broker working for the broker. In the real estate business, the salesperson or associate broker may refer to it as "my listing," but it isn't. The salesperson or associate broker is acting as agent of the broker, so the broker is really the sellers' agent. If the sellers have a problem, they need to call the broker.

In similar fashion, if you hire a buyer's agent, you may be dealing with a salesperson or associate broker, but your "agent" is really the broker they are working for. Think of it this way — you are hiring the company, although you deal with the company through its agent. The sellers do the same thing when they list their property.

Seller agency

In the past a buyer wouldn't have had much choice in the matter of representation. All real estate agents took listings from the sellers, which automatically obligated the company to represent the sellers. That's what the listing contract does — by signing it the sellers hire the broker as their agent. Buyers represented themselves. Let's look at how things used to work back then (and still work in the majority of transactions today).

A real estate agent (salesperson or associate broker working for a real estate broker) goes out and takes a listing from the seller. The salespersons and associate brokers are agents of the broker, empowered by the broker to conduct business in the broker's name. The sellers have hired the broker to sell their property.

The broker also authorizes salespersons and associate brokers to show and sell property to buyers. Although you might be dealing with a different salesperson or associate broker than the agent who took the listing, the agent you are dealing with is still representing the broker, and therefore the sellers. This is a little confusing for someone outside the real estate field, so look at the drawing below to see how it works.

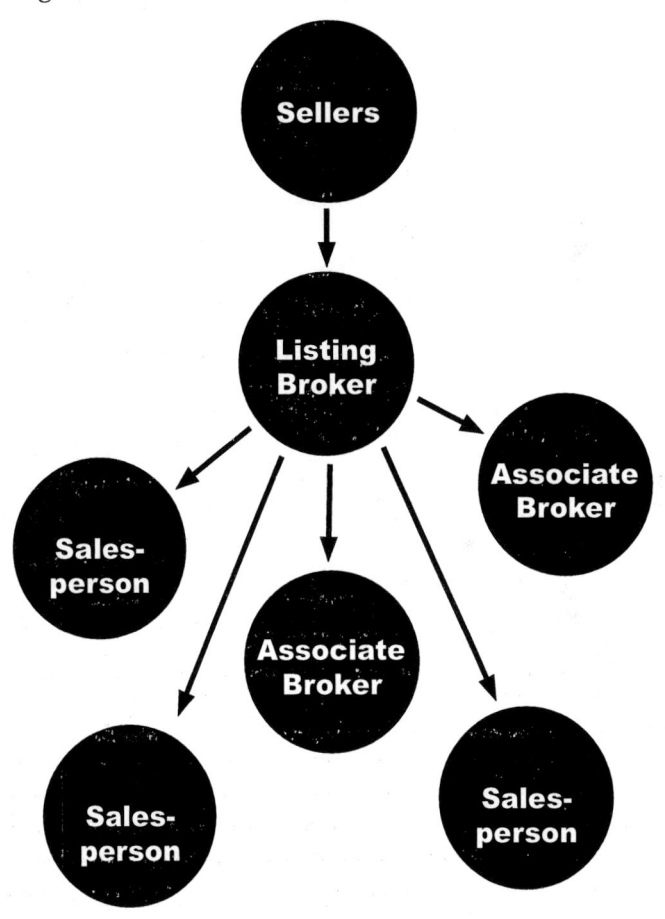

```
              Sellers
                 |
                 v
           Listing Broker
          /    |       \
         /     |        \
        v      v         v
   Sales-  Associate   Associate
   person   Broker      Broker
             / \
            /   \
           v     v
        Sales-  Sales-
        person  person
```

Note that everyone is representing the sellers. No one is representing you. You are representing yourself. Feel kind of left out? You should. To borrow an old expression from lawyers, when you represent yourself you have a fool for a client. We'll deal with this in a bit, so bear with me.

When an agent shows a property listed by another company, the relationships get more involved. Now the selling company and their agents become agents of the listing company.

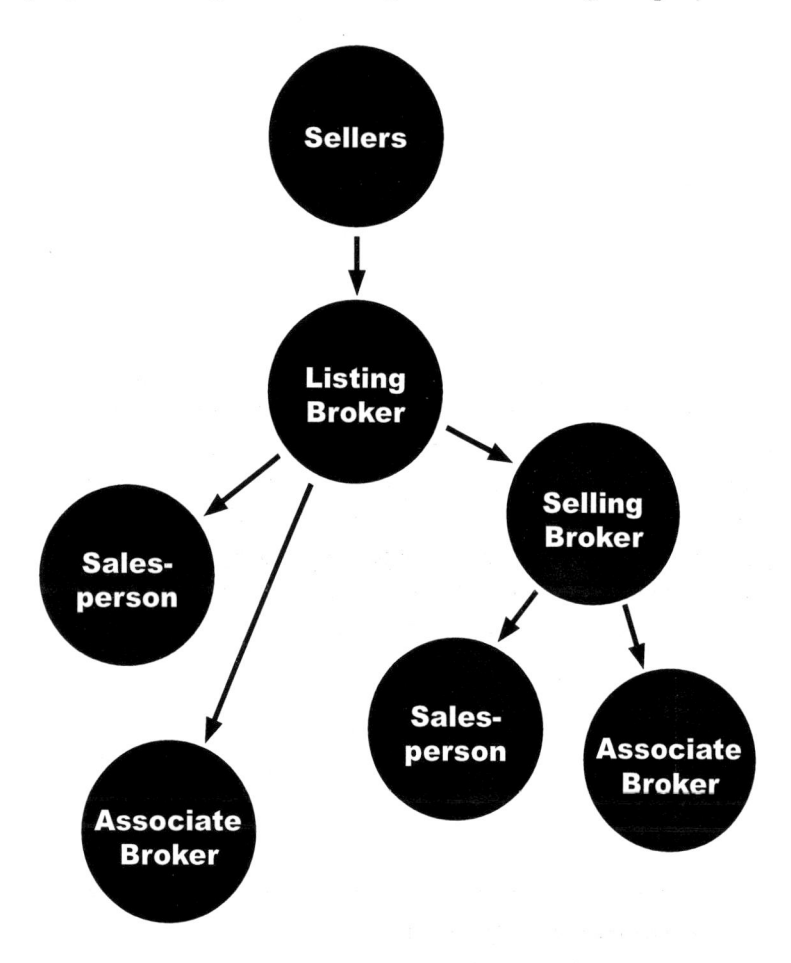

```
                    Sellers
                       │
                       ▼
                   Listing
                   Broker
              ┌───────┼───────┐
              ▼       │       ▼
          Sales-      │    Selling
          person      │    Broker
                      │   ┌───┴───┐
                      ▼   ▼       ▼
                  Associate Sales-  Associate
                  Broker    person  Broker
```

Agents of other agents are called subagents. The term is really unimportant, because ultimately the chain leads to the principal. A broker's instructions to his or her agents is to do whatever the principal needs, so the principal is still the boss. Nevertheless, some people use the term "subagency" as a synonym for a relationship where the agents are representing the seller. This is really kind of inaccurate, because an agent representing a buyer can have subagents as well. The term "subagent" just means "agent of another agent."

Notice that there are no buyers in either of the drawings above. That's because so far none of the agents are representing the buyers yet. The buyers are still representing themselves.

Buyer agency

Fifteen years ago, for a real estate agent to represent a buyer in a residential sale was so uncommon that many real estate agents had never heard of the idea. Today things are very different, indeed. While the majority of sales are still conducted with all agents representing the seller, buyer agency has also become very common.

In the drawing below, notice how buyer agency creates two paths — each side in the transaction has a separate agent.

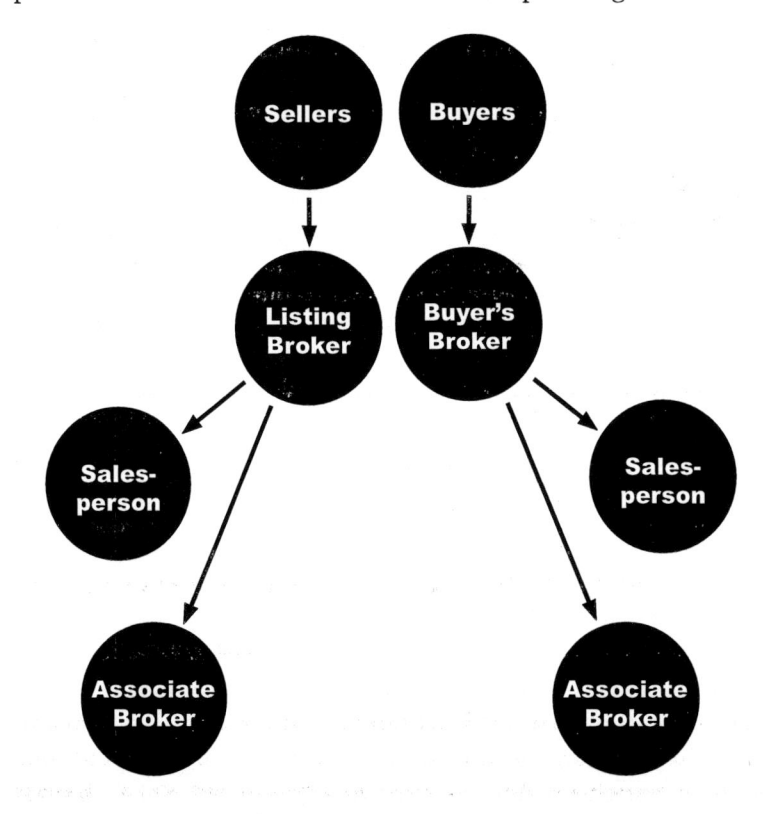

Needless to say, if you are an intelligent buyer you will probably want a buyer's agent. But the important thing to note is that *unless there is some specific agreement in writing to the contrary, the agent you are talking to is representing the sellers.*

Dual agency

Dual agency is where the agent represents both parties. This is kind of tricky. After all, how can an agent owe both full disclosure and confidentiality to both parties at the same time? If you tell a dual agent how high you will go, the agent owes you the duty to keep that confidential, but at the same time owes a duty to the seller to disclose it. This creates an impossible situation. The law gets around that by compromising — the agent in a dual agency is permitted to keep confidentialities from both sides. Other fiduciary obligations are also modified slightly. "Loyalty" becomes "equal loyalty," for example.

Remember, if an agent represents the buyer or the seller exclusively, this is called single agency (because there is only one principal). Dual agency is the third possibility. Although less common, dual agency does occur on occasion. Suppose, for example, you are being represented by a buyer's agent. This agent also takes listings. And suddenly, you are interested in seeing a property that your agent has listed personally. Being the listing agent means your agent is already the agent of the seller, but if the agent has also agreed to be your buyer's agent, then the agent has two masters at the same time. There is only one out. To show you that property the agent must become a dual agent for that transaction.

Agency disclosure

But how do you know whether the agent is representing you, the seller, or both of you? In the past this was a perennial problem. Today the issue is a lot clearer because the law now requires the agent to give you an agency disclosure statement. The statement will make it clear whose side the agent is on.

While both Oregon and Washington require the agent to

disclose, there is a difference in each state's requirements. In Oregon the law requires the agent to give you a prescribed agency disclosure form "at or before the first substantive contact" [ORS 696.820 (5)]. This means as soon as you start discussing your real estate needs with the agent or ask for information about a property. The agent is required to get your signature on a form and give you a copy of it.

This works well, because you know right up front whose side the agent is on. In Washington, however, at the beginning of the relationship the agent is not required to give you anything at all. The actual disclosure of who the agent is working for doesn't need to be made until it's time to sign the earnest money form (offer to buy). At that time the disclosure must be made and the agent must give the principal a pamphlet describing the law of agency [RCW 18.86.030 (1)(g)]. You could be dealing with a seller's agent, yet be thinking the agent is representing you. You might not discover your error until you make an offer to buy a property. And even then the actual disclosure is in the fine print on the purchase agreement, so a lot of buyers might not notice it. Better have it out with the agent up front if you want to be sure the agent is representing you as a buyer's agent.

As in Oregon, there are plenty of Washington agents who openly advertise themselves as buyers' agents. These agents usually have a disclosure form they use up front voluntarily. Just because Washington law does not require them to disclose until the point where you make an offer to buy a house doesn't mean they can't voluntarily disclose up front. If an agent doesn't disclose at the first meeting, by all means ask. If you don't know whose side the agent is on, it's probably not yours. Better to know for sure.

If you are in Oregon, the agency disclosure form for a buyer's agent is on the following pages. If you are working with an agent in Oregon and the agent has not given you the agency disclosure form, not only are they breaking the law, but they are a major slacker to be avoided at all costs!

Before I leave this area, I must mention that there is one other term you will encounter — the "exclusive buyer's agent." Remember I said above that some agents take listings only, some

BUYER'S AGENCY DISCLOSURE ACKNOWLEDGMENT
INITIAL ACKNOWLEDGMENT OF PROSPECTIVE BUYER

By my signature below, I acknowledge:

(1) I have received and read and I understand the material set out on the back of this disclosure form.

(2) I understand that a seller's agent, including a listing agent, is the agent of the seller exclusively, unless the seller and the buyer otherwise agree.

(3) I understand that, unless otherwise disclosed in writing, all real estate licensees including real estate licensees participating in a multiple listing service are agents of the seller exclusively.

(4) I understand that I may engage my own agent to be my buyer's agent.

(5) I understand that _____
(name of licensee) of _____
(name of real estate organization), the agent presenting this form to me, is (check applicable relationship):

_____ an agent of the seller.

_____ my agent as buyer's agent.

BUYER'S LIMITED AUTHORIZATION REGARDING IN-COMPANY SALES

By my initials below, I acknowledge:

(1) A situation may arise wherein the licensee I have hired to be my agent may also be the agent for the seller of specific real property I wish to acquire.

(2) If this situation arises, I authorize my agent to act as an in-company agent for that specific real property after making a reasonably diligent effort to contact me in order to obtain my consent.

(3) I have read and understand the "In-Company Sales" section on the reverse side of this form.

(4) The following information, which has previously been disclosed by the buyer to the agent, is confidential and is not to be disclosed to the seller.

UNDERSTOOD AND AGREED:

_____   _____ (Initials)

SIGNATURES
Buyer: _____ Dated: _____
Buyer: _____ Dated: _____
Buyer: _____ Dated: _____
Buyer: _____ Dated: _____

AGENT TO SIGN AND DATE:

_____ Real Estate Licensee
_____ Real Estate Organization

DISCLOSURE REGARDING AGENCY RELATIONSHIP(S)
(As required by Oregon Revised Statutes Chapter 696)
An agency relationship arises whenever two persons agree that one is to act on behalf of the other and in accordance with the other's directions. The creation of an agency relationship imposes certain legal duties on the agent. Before a seller or a buyer enters into a discussion with a real estate licensee regarding a real property transaction, the seller and the buyer should each understand what type of agency relationship or representation the buyer and the seller may have with each agent in that transaction.

SELLER'S AGENT
An agent who acts under a listing agreement with the seller acts as the agent for the seller only. A seller's agent has affirmative obligations (under ORS 696.805):
(1) To the seller: The fiduciary duties of loyalty, obedience, disclosure, confidentiality, reasonable care and diligence, and accounting in dealings with the seller.
(2) To the buyer and to the seller: Honest dealing and disclosure.

BUYER'S AGENT
A real estate licensee other than the seller's agent can agree with the buyer to act as the agent for the buyer only. In this situation, the buyer's agent is not representing the seller, even if the buyer's agent is receiving compensation for services rendered, either in full or in part, from the seller or through the seller's agent. A buyer's agent has the affirmative obligations (under ORS 696.810):
(1) To the buyer: The fiduciary duties of loyalty, obedience, disclosure, confidentiality, reasonable care and diligence, and accounting in dealings with the buyer.
(2) To the buyer and to the seller: Honest dealing and disclosure.

IN-COMPANY SALES
(1) A licensee, acting either alone or through one or more licensees within the same real estate organization, may give limited representation to both the seller and the buyer in a real estate transaction.
(2) In an in-company agreement, the agent acting as an in-company agent has the following affirmative obligations to both the seller and the buyer:
(a) Loyalty, obedience, disclosure, confidentiality and accounting in dealings with both the seller and the buyer. **HOWEVER, IN REPRESENTING BOTH THE SELLER AND THE BUYER, THE LICENSEE SHALL NOT, WITHOUT THE EXPRESS WRITTEN PERMISSION OF THE RESPECTIVE PERSON, DISCLOSE TO THE OTHER PERSON:**
(i) That the seller will accept a price lower than or terms less favorable than the listing price or terms; or
(ii) That the buyer will pay a price higher than or terms more favorable than the offering price and terms; or
(iii) Other than price and terms, confidential information specifically designated as such in writing by the buyer or seller as set out on the front of this disclosure form or attached to it.
(b) Reasonable care and diligence.
(c) Honest dealing.

SELLERS AND BUYERS
None of the foregoing duties of the agent in a real estate transaction relieves a seller or a buyer from the responsibility to protect the seller's or buyer's own interests respectively. The seller and the buyer should carefully read all agreements to assure that the agreements adequately express the seller's or the buyer's understanding of the transaction.

THE ACTS OF THE AGENTS MAY CAUSE LEGAL LIABILITY TO THE PRINCIPALS. A REAL ESTATE LICENSEE IS QUALIFIED TO ADVISE ON REAL ESTATE; IF YOU DESIRE LEGAL ADVICE, CONSULT A LAWYER.

represent buyers only, and some do either, depending on which way the wind is blowing that day. An "exclusive buyer's agent" is an agent who never takes listings. As a matter of principle, the exclusive buyer's agent only works with buyers.

In theory, it shouldn't matter if you use a buyer's agent who also takes listings now and then. The only time there would be a problem is if you want to see one of your agent's personal listings, which isn't all that likely. But in the real world you will find that agents who work exclusively as buyer's agents take the issue of buyer agency very seriously. You will find that they are far more knowledgeable about buyer agency. They have experience in representing buyers which will be invaluable to you. It shouldn't come as any surprise then when I say that I strongly urge you to obtain the services of an exclusive buyer's agent.

Now that we have the basic idea of who is representing whom, there is another very important consideration regarding the law of agency — that is, the party paying the commission is not necessarily the principal. You are the principal if the agent has agreed to represent you. If the agent is getting a commission from the seller only, this does not mean the agent can't be representing you exclusively. The agent represents whichever party is named in the agency disclosure statement whether it is given up front or on the earnest money form. Who the agent is being paid by is irrelevant.

Does that mean that, if you use a buyer's agent, you will be expected to pay the agent a commission? Yikes! There goes the down payment money! Well, not necessarily. Before we get into that we need to consider another aspect of the real estate business — commissions.

How agents get paid

In residential transactions these days the commission is usually a percentage of the sales price, ranging from three or four percent to seven or eight percent or so. The percentage varies from company to company and according to the price of the house (i.e., a lower percentage for a more expensive home). There are also agents who charge according to how much service the agent is going to perform — e.g., "for sale by owner" service companies who let the seller do some of the work in exchange for a reduced commission. And if that isn't confusing enough, there are even some agents who work on a flat fee basis.

Let's put some numbers to this to see what it means in terms of real money. A first-time buyer in the northwest would probably be looking for a house these days in the $100,000 to $150,000 range, so let's assume a sales price of $125,000. A typical commission rate would be about six percent, so that means a total commission of $7,500.

Sounds like a lot for very little work, doesn't it? Well, before you decide that real estate sales is a great way to get rich quick, let's bring that figure down to earth. The first problem is that the agent doesn't get the whole commission. The broker takes a healthy whack off the top to cover company overhead and profit. And then the selling agent probably has to split the commission with the listing agent. In most areas the listing agent and the selling agent each get about half of the amount remaining after the broker's share. If the selling agent ends up with $2,500 out of that $7,500, that would be typical.

Not only that, if the agent sells another company's listing, then the commission is fragmented even further because the commission is first split between the listing and selling companies (called a "co-op" commission). And out of whatever the agent nets, the agent has to pay hundreds of dollars a month in expenses — multiple listing fees, membership dues, car expenses, signs, lockboxes — the list goes on and on. If there's still anything left, Uncle Sam will take his share too.

The amount of commission, as well as how the commissions are split is set by negotiation between the parties. If anyone attempted to require all agents to use the same splits or percentages it would be in restraint of trade and a violation of federal law (price-fixing). You can be assured that there is never a "standard fee" that everyone charges. All agents' fees are always negotiable. If an agent ever tries to tell you otherwise, dump that agent pronto.

Now that you have an idea of how an agent is paid, let's go back to the problem of working with a buyer's agent without having to pay a huge chunk of your limited cash on the agent's fee. There is nothing in the law which prohibits a buyer's agent from accepting a part of the commission paid by the seller. In other words, your buyer's agent can get paid the same co-op commission as if he or she was working strictly for the seller. Remember, what establishes who the agent represents is the written disclosure statement, not who is paying the agent.

Unfortunately, this doesn't work out well in every case. What if you are working with a buyer's agent, you spend weeks looking at homes, and then never buy anything at all? A few buyer's agents try to avoid working completely for free by asking buyers to agree to pay the agent an hourly fee. Most agree that, if you do buy, and the agent does get a portion of the commission paid by the seller, then you won't have to pay the hourly charge.

But what if you are working with a buyer's agent and you end up wanting to buy a house that is not listed (a for sale by owner)? Most buyer's agents expect you to pay them a fee in that case. However, you may not necessarily have to. It's possible that your agent can negotiate a fee from the sellers. Remember, your buyer's agent is expecting to be paid only about half the typical commission, so the sellers will be asked to pay a lot less than if they had listed the property. Maybe they'll agree to it. If they won't then you'll probably be expected to pay your agent yourself.

Today there are other problems. In the metropolitan areas the most common full commission is 6%. It is not unusual for a listing agent to take a listing with the understanding that the listing agent will get 3% and the seller will pay a buyer's agent only a flat fee of $500 or $1,000. If your buyer's agency agreement calls for your agent to get 3%, this isn't going to cover what you owe your agent (3% of a typical sales price of $125,000 would be $3,750). How can you buy this house? The same as with the for sale by owner, your agent will have to try to ask the sellers to raise the amount they will pay, or you will have to pay the difference out of pocket.

Why would a listing agent take a listing on such terms? The answer is very simple — to get the listing. There is intense competition among real estate companies for listings. The listing agent is using a lower commission rate as a gimmick to get the listing. For the sellers it is probably a false economy, but they don't know that. After all, because they refuse to pay a buyer's agent, many buyers will pass them by. The sellers are just looking at "3% + $500" vs. 6% and went with the cheaper option. They're really hurting themselves, but until they figure it out there isn't much you can do.

To ensure that they will be paid, buyer's agents frequently ask buyers to sign a "buyer listing agreement." This agreement usually says that you will pay the agent if you buy a property within a certain number of months. The agreement is generally exclusive, i.e., you agree that you will not engage the services of any other buyer's agents.

Be very careful with buyer agency agreements! Make sure you understand exactly under what circumstances you will be obligated to pay a buyer's agent fee. You want a buyer's agent, but you want the seller to pay your agent. You should also insist on the right to cancel the agency agreement. Not only are agent's fees always negotiable, but the rest of the terms of the agreement are as well. A professional agent will explain the terms of a buyer's agency agreement, and will be willing to discuss modifications to meet your particular needs. Remember, this person is going to be your employee, so there is every reason to make the relationship one that you are both comfortable with.

As buyer agency grows in popularity, the terms of buyer agency agreements keep changing. Personally, there is something about the way buyer agents currently get paid that doesn't set right with me — they are paid a percentage of the sales price. Therefore, the more you pay, the more your agent earns.

While this is a holdover from the days when everyone represented the sellers, it doesn't make any sense to me. If I am being represented by an agent, I want the agent to earn more if I pay *less*. I have heard of at least a few agents who are taking this to heart and making a different arrangement. One agent I ran into was charging 2½% of the listed price, plus 10% of what the buyer ended up paying *under* than the listed price. I thought this was a fair arrangement — the buyer's agent has a motivation to get a good price for the buyer.

Yet when I called an exclusive buyer's agent and asked for

this arrangement she flat refused. According to her, that would introduce a "sleaze factor" which she didn't feel was professional. She felt that she did a good job for her buyers without adding a financial incentive. She was afraid that it would make buyer's agents and seller's agents too cutthroat, to the ultimate detriment of their clients.

Should you insist on a commission arrangement that rewards your agent financially according to how well you do? I can say that getting an agent to agree to it is not going to be easy in today's real estate market because agents are not yet accustomed to it. But I do feel that it will eventually become the norm. In the meantime, just because your agent is not financially rewarded according to how well you do, doesn't mean your agent isn't doing an excellent job for you. Most buyer's agents are very conscientious about their duty to their buyers, regardless of how they are getting paid. It's something you need to discuss openly with your agent and be sure you and the agent are both comfortable with what you expect of each other. The one sure way to lose, however, is to fail to discuss the agent's compensation openly with the agent.

While we're talking about commissions, there are some other important considerations. Almost all real estate agents work exclusively on commission. It is virtually unheard of for a real estate company to pay a sales agent a salary. If the agent makes no sales, the agent's family doesn't eat. You're probably thinking "that's all very nice, but why should I care?" You care because if you waste an agent's time, you are going to get poor service. Agents can't afford to spend time with tire-kickers. When you first meet an agent you can expect to be grilled about your home-buying plans and qualifications. It would be a waste of the agent's time to show you houses that didn't fit your needs, or that were too expensive for your budget. There is only one way for the agent to get that information, and that is to get you to open up and tell all. Give an agent the silent treatment and you are likely to be shown the door.

Of course, the above applies only to your own agent. While you must be open with a buyer's agent, the opposite is true when speaking to other agents. You don't want them passing on infor-

Chapter 2, *Gypsies, Tramps and Thieves* 35

mation to the other side that would compromise your negotiations. Still, they are trained to persist in getting information. One advantage of working with an exclusive buyer's agent is that you can just say "I'm already working with an exclusive buyer's agent." That phrase will stop all other agents dead in their tracks.

Of course, there may be cases where you can work just as effectively with a sellers' (listing) agent. Every situation is unique and it's hard to make hard and fast rules. Buying a property directly through the listing agent has one advantage — the commission is not split as much. The listing agent gets the listing commission and the sales commission as well. This can motivate the agent to get your offer accepted. Still, the listing agent owes no duties to you. As desirable as it would be to get your offer accepted, the listing agent's primary duty is to get you to pay as much as possible. And never forget that the agent for the seller owes the seller the duty of full disclosure — whatever beans you spill to the sellers' agent are going to be passed on to the sellers.

Finding the right agent

It should be clear by now that you want to work with a buyer's agent, preferably an exclusive buyer's agent. But how do you find the right agent? It would appear that you want a broker, right? After all, the broker is the top gun. But in many real estate companies the broker spends all day running the business, not out selling real estate. In the trade, these are called "non-competing brokers" — because they do not "compete" with the salespersons for sales. This is typical of most big real estate companies. In smaller companies you may find the broker is more a jack of all trades.

And that brings up a related issue — should you seek an agent in a large company or a small one? Well, first, many large companies are not really large companies, but in fact are locally owned franchises. Many of the big names in real estate are really operated this way — Century 21, Coldwell Banker, RE/MAX and Prudential, among others. And some companies own most of the offices, but allow a few of them to be operated as franchises. Yet other large companies are really single, large brokerage firms where none of the offices are franchises.

It doesn't really matter, though. The answer to the large company vs. small company question is really six of one and half a dozen of the other. Agents in bigger companies may have more resources available to serve their customers, but may be less flexible. From a buyer's perspective, the personality and experience of the individual agent is far more important than the size of the company he or she works for.

But getting back to finding the right buyer's agent, unless you are working with a very small company, you probably won't be working directly with the broker. Should you settle for an associate broker then? Well, there is one real advantage to using an associate broker — it takes extra experience and education to get the associate brokers license, so you know you are dealing with someone who considers real estate a career and is not just brand new in the business. But, frankly, a salesperson can sometimes be better. After all, it's not the title after the name that matters; it's hard work, experience, ability and attitude that make the difference.

How about an agent who is a top producer? You see these

agents frequently featured in company ads in the local paper — their photos with their sales volume captioned underneath. Or their business card may say they are members of the "Million Dollar Club." Would such an agent make a good buyer's agent?

The answer is a definite maybe. The problem with top producers is that, in the real estate field, it takes really hard work to be a top producer. There is an old saying in the sales field — the top 20% do 80% of the business, and the bottom 80% account for the remaining 20% of sales. Agents who are top producers must be pretty ruthless with their time. They dash from appointment to appointment, slaves to their schedule. This produces high commissions, but their clients may find them difficult to get hold of. Don't expect them to want to take time to hold your hand. Of course, high producers also go after the more expensive properties, so it's not likely they would be very interested in a typical first-time buyer anyway.

These days it seems everybody and his dog has a real estate license. You may already have a friend who is an agent. If the friend has been in the business long enough, you may have an excellent agent. But beware of the beginner. You want someone experienced at negotiating, and it takes years to learn that. Probably the worst thing you can do is help a friend trying to get into the business. It sounds harsh to say that, but it's reality.

Even if your friend in the business is experienced, you may be well advised to look elsewhere. Under the best of conditions, buying a house is a stressful process. More than one friendship has ended up on the rocks over a real estate transaction. How much do you value your friendship?

If you're having a hard time figuring out how to get out of using your friend gracefully, blame this book. Just say "I read a book for first-time buyers and it said using a friend in the business is a good way to lose a friend." Now what friend could be angry with you after that?

Another type of agent to avoid is one who doesn't work on the type of property you are looking for. If you need to be located in the city, don't hook up with an agent in the country. And be sure your agent is a residential agent, preferably one who specializes in your price range. There are all kinds of real estate agents out there — industrial agents, office leasing agents, investment brokers, and so on. Don't expect any of these to have a clue about finding you a house, or even knowing how to fill out the earnest money agreement for it.

You should also steer clear of part-timers. Unfortunately, the real estate field is full of part-time agents. And equally unfortunately, there is no easy way to spot them short of asking them straight out. Obviously, you need a professional, full-time agent, so plan on asking before you agree to let the agent represent you.

A good agent will educate you about the market. Actually, you can do a lot of this yourself. Start by checking the ads in the local paper and driving by the listings. It takes several tanks of gas, but eventually you will get a feel for property values. Don't expect to stumble across a steal; they don't exist. A steal is never going to last long enough to make it into the paper. Instead, look at properties with the idea of learning what properties are worth. The best appraisers all admit that appraising is an art, not a science. You can get a pretty good feel by doing the groundwork yourself. At this stage you are not seriously trying to buy; you're just getting an education. The most educated buyer is one who looks at 50 houses all listed at exactly the same price. This will make you the most knowledgeable person in town at that price. When faced with houses in that price range, you will know value when you see it.

Although you can teach yourself to a large extent, your agent should share with you his or her knowledge of neighborhoods, appreciation rates, average sales prices, and other data. Most of this information is public, but your agent can help you locate it and save you time. An agent will also educate you about local terminology and never talk over your head. For example, in some areas when a buyer offers to buy a property and take over the seller's old loan, we say the transaction was "cash to the loan." In other areas the term is "assumption." Your agent should make sure you understand the terminology. For your part, never fail to pipe up when you don't understand something.

One of the most important services your agent should provide you is information about financing. Yes, you can (and should) get preapproved by a lender. But which lender? There are some real sharks out there in the lending field these days. Steering you into safe waters is one of your agent's most important duties.

Your agent should never make decisions for you. It is one thing to give you advice. It is quite another to push you into something. Remember, if you're working with a buyer's agent, the agent is your employee. You're the boss. Act like one. If you're not comfortable with the agent, don't sign a buyer's agency agreement with that agent.

While all the above are important things the agent should do for you, remember that the primary thing you need is a good negotiator. You want someone who knows how to present your offer and get it accepted. This is difficult to evaluate objectively in an agent, but you can still get a good feel just by chatting with the agent. Don't be in a rush to jump into an agency relationship. An agent with the gift of gab that you are looking for will reveal himself or herself to you fairly soon if you just listen.

Recommended minimum acceptable standards —
- A buyer's agent who can show you at the first meeting a list of 25 houses in your price range that have been on the market for 90 days or more
- An agent with a minimum of 50 closed transactions representing buyers
- An agent who understands that your interests are more important than the agent's commission
- *Bonus:* An agent who agrees to a compensation arrangement where the agent earns more the better you do

---

So now that you know what kind of agent you are looking for, how do you find him or her? Well, that's the easy part. Just call a real estate company and ask about a house they have advertised. If it's during normal business hours, usually you will get the secretary, who will turn you over to the salesperson on the floor. "On the floor" is sales jargon for the agent who is currently supposed to take all new leads. ("Floor time is also sometimes called "up time.")

Agents go through sales training to learn how to handle the telephone, so you can expect the agent will start right out by asking you what you are looking for, how much you want to spend, and so on. The agent is going for your phone number and an appointment to meet you, and you are usually going for the address of the property, or some other information about it. There is nothing wrong with letting the agent have his or her way — after all, this may turn out to be just the agent you are looking for.

Unfortunately, you want an experienced agent, and experienced agents hate "floor time." They usually have all the clients they need and are not interested in warming a chair in the office in case someone calls. But that doesn't mean that the person you are talking to is not the right one. It just means that you may have to make appointments with numerous agents before you find one you are satisfied with.

We should also add that many companies no longer have floor time. All calls about a property are turned over to the agent who listed the property. This doesn't matter — the listing agent may turn out to be the one you are looking for too. Just because an agent takes listings doesn't mean the agent doesn't also act as a buyer's broker from time to time. This is especially true in smaller communities.

One excellent way to find a good buyer's agent is to look for ads in local "homes for sale" publications (the kind that are on display in restaurants and motel lobbies) or the homes for sale section of the local paper. There are many agents who work exclusively as buyer's agents. Since they don't have listings, there is no way for them to snare clients by sitting in the office. They have no alternative but to run ads announcing their services.

Probably the best way to find a buyer's agent is to get a referral from a buyer who used that agent and was happy with the service. If you have any friends who recently bought a home, check with them and see if they used a buyer's agent.

If you can't get a referral another excellent way to find a professional buyer's agent is to check with Real Estate Buyers Agent Council of the National Association of Realtors® or with the National Association of Exclusive Buyer Agents. Both of these organizations are listed in the Resources section at the end of this book, together with addresses, phone numbers and their web sites.

Buying from a for sale by owner without an agent
Don't.

Ok, there may be exceptions, but they are rare. First, let's consider what kind of sellers would sell by owner instead of listing with an agent. ("For sale by owner" is usually abbreviated to "FSBO," and is pronounced "fizz-bow.") The FSBO's usual motivation is to save the commission. Well, guess what? That's what you want to do too. But there's only one commission to save, so automatically you are in a tug of war with the sellers.

Experienced investors know that for sale by owners overprice the property, are impossible to negotiate with, and are so tight they squeak. They are better left to their own devices.

But that's not all. The typical for sale by owner knows little more than you do about buying or selling a home. You have no one to explain things to you, no one to guide you to the right lender, no one to make sure you are not paying fees you shouldn't be paying — you are lost in space. And you should hope that the seller is equally unsophisticated, because, if the seller is a veteran at selling homes, you are at a serious disadvantage.

One agent I know calls FSBOs "unconscious incompetents." They don't know what they are talking about, but they don't know they don't know.

Another agent says "if you absolutely must have more than your house is worth, then the for sale by owner marketplace may get it for you." Yet another says "the unknowledgeable buyer is like a deer in the FSBO's headlights and the state should issue tags to predatory FSBOs so as to limit them to two in a lifetime."

If you still want to buy a FSBO, there is the problem of negotiating. The nice thing about real estate agents is that they act as go-betweens. Some people are great at negotiating for themselves. Most of us, however, feel shy and find it really hard to press for what we want when we are face to face with the other party. Can you make a seller a low offer without trembling? Are you skilled enough that you can do so without getting the seller angry? Not that an agent will always be successful at these things either, but it sure helps to have a mediator.

That having been said, there are occasional advantages to dealing with a for sale by owner. One is when you have little or no money and/or questionable credit. For sale by owners very commonly agree to carry the financing themselves. You can find properties listed with agents where the seller will carry the financing too, but now the seller needs a down payment at least large enough to cover the agent's commission. A FSBO is more likely to agree to a lower down payment.

Nevertheless, this is an area for extreme caution. There are investor barracudas in residential real estate waters. A common practice is to buy a shabby house, give it a cosmetic treatment, double the price, and sell it for little or nothing down. The investor is hoping to attract a buyer stupid enough to be wowed by a fresh coat of paint and willing to pay an inflated price. Unfortunately, they are often successful. Don't be their next victim.

How do you know when you are dealing with a seller like this? If you're in doubt, there is one way you may be able to find out for sure. Call your local title insurance company and ask for the Customer Service Department. Tell them you want to know how many properties this person has bought in the past couple of years, the purchase price, and how many the person has sold and the sales price. All deeds must be filed in the public records and must state the true and actual consideration. The names of the buyer and seller are maintained in an index, so the data is easy to look up. Title insurance companies provide the service free in most areas of the northwest. If you are in an area where they want to charge, then you can get the same information for free from the county recorder's office, although you may have to go to their office in person and do the research yourself.

Another way is to call the state agency that licenses builders. People who fix up houses for resale are required to be registered in both Oregon and Washington (unless they live in the property). There is no regulation as to the quality of work they do — other than local building codes — but at least you can find out if they are regularly engaged in the business of fixing up houses for resale. And if they're doing it and not registered, then they're acting illegally and to be avoided at all costs.

Of course, such an investigation is probably not necessary. It's usually pretty obvious. If you've done your homework, you'll already know the property is overpriced. And then too, most of us can smell the special odor this kind of seller gives off.

Buying a new home

Large builders usually have their own sales staff. Their properties are not generally listed with a real estate agent, so if you have a buyer's agent, and want to buy a new house, you'll have to decide how to compensate your agent. On the other hand, smaller builders either sell their properties themselves, or list them with real estate companies. If they are listed, your buyer's agent can probably get a co-op commission the same as any other listed property. If the builder does all the sales work alone without a sales staff or listing them, then you have to treat the builder as any other for sale by owner — i.e., compensating your agent becomes an issue again.

Occasionally you will find a builder who generally sells the properties without listing them, but might advertise "broker participation," or use the older term "courtesy to brokers." These phrases mean that the builder will pay a commission to an agent if the agent brings a buyer, but will not sign a listing with any agent.

One thing to consider about builders is that they typically have five or six months' carrying charges (interest) on their construction loan built into the sales price. If you buy right at the moment the house is completed, you may be able to negotiate a price lower by this amount. This can come to several thousand dollars. Consider that a builder may be paying 9% interest on a construction loan of $100,000 or so. The monthly interest would be $750, so five or six months' worth would come to $3,750 to $4,500 — certainly an amount worth considering when you make an offer.

Listings

Although buyers are certainly not going to be signing a listing agreement, you should be aware that there are different kinds of listings. By far the most common is the *exclusive right to sell listing*, usually just called an "exclusive" listing for short. When sellers gives an exclusive right to sell listing to an agent, they promise to pay the commission if a sale is brought about any time during the term of the listing, regardless of who sells the property. Even if the sellers find the buyer, the agent is entitled to the commission. Almost all listings today are exclusive right to sell listings. Any listing in the multiple listing service is undoubtedly an exclusive right to sell listing.

And just in case there is a bit of larceny in your heart, take note that the seller owes the commission if a sale is brought about even after the listing expires — if the sale is made to someone the broker introduced the property to during the term of the listing. This is commonly called the "safety" or "extender" clause. Agents put this clause is in their listing to make sure unethical buyers and sellers don't conspire to wait out the listing and avoid the commission.

On rare occasions you may encounter an *exclusive agency listing*. The exclusive agency listing means that the seller reserves the right to sell the property without owing a commission. It is an "exclusive agency" because the seller does agree not to give listings to other agents.

You may also encounter an *open listing*, also called a *non-exclusive listing*. This is the least restrictive for the seller. The seller can sell the property without being liable for a commission, and can give additional open listings to other agents. Whichever agent brings about a sale is entitled to the full commission and none of the other agents get anything. Open listings are usually given by government agencies to market surplus properties. The agency will mail copies of the listing en masse to all brokers in the area. Such listings are usually ignored by agents. About the only time an agent will get excited about an open listing is if a buyer calls up and asks to be shown the property. Certainly the agent isn't going to spend his or her own money advertising a property with no prospect of getting at least the listing share of the commission.

A "multiple listing" isn't really a type of listing, but rather, refers to a listing that has been placed in the multiple listing service (MLS). Just about every community has an MLS. The MLS is frequently run by the local board of Realtors®, but in some communities may be run by the local brokers separately from the board. Agents join the MLS in order to participate in each other's listings.

Here's how the MLS works. A seller gives an exclusive right to sell listing to a particular real estate company (broker). The company is a member of the MLS, whose rules require submission of all new listings within a certain time limit (usually 24 hours or so). The listings are then available for all members to show. The company who listed the property stipulates how much commission the selling company will receive if they are successful in finding a buyer.

The MLS has extensive rules for how brokers are to cooperate with each other. For example, if an agent wants to show another broker's listing, usually the agent is first to look for special instructions in the listing data, but if no instructions, then is to call the seller first for an appointment. If an offer is written, the selling agent must call the listing company to let them know that an offer has been written. The agent is usually required to present it with a representative of the listing company present. (In some communities the rule is that the selling agent is to go directly to the seller, but that is the exception.) There are many other such rules defining inter-company protocols, all designed to make sure agents and their clients are treated fairly.

The MLS also provides certain other services to its members. For example, the MLS makes available lockboxes. Lockboxes are little metal boxes that can be locked onto the house and which every agent has a key to. Inside the lockbox the listing agent places the house key. If it weren't for lockboxes the agents would always have to run over to the listing agent's office to pick up the key, then run back and return it after showing — obviously a major pain.

You may run into a "one-party listing" from time to time. This isn't really a legal type of listing — the legal forms are the exclusive right to sell, exclusive agency and open. A one-party listing can be any of these, but is usually exclusive right to sell. In fact, it is identical to a regular listing, except that the agent writes in the margin somewhere that the listing is valid only for a particular buyer.

The one party listing arises once in a while when an agent is out prospecting for new listings. The minute a for sale by owner puts an ad in the paper the phone will start ringing. Half the calls will be real estate agents soliciting the listing. A common line the agent will use is "I have someone who I think would be very interested in your property." Now, any agent actively selling real estate has lots of buyer prospects, and surely one of them would be interested, so it's not really a lie. To get rid of them, the savvy seller will say, "no I don't want to tie myself up, but if you have someone you want to show the property to, I will give you a one-party listing." The purpose is to get rid of the agent, but once in a while the agent really does have a hot prospect, and may actually end up taking the one-party listing and showing the property.

You should also be aware that the agent is free to show any property, with or without a prior listing. The license laws and the NAR Code of Ethics do not require that there be a listing before showing the property. The problem is that the agent cannot legally enforce collection of a commission without a written listing agreement or commission agreement. Therefore, if the agent shows you a property without something signed by the seller agreeing to pay the agent's fee, he or she is depending on the seller's good faith. It's possible for the seller to say, "sure I'll accept the offer, but I'm not signing any agreement to pay the commission." As a result, you can expect a certain resistance to showing properties without first meeting with the seller and getting at least a fee agreement in writing.

What if you have a problem with an agent?

The first thing to do is discuss it with the agent. While this may sound obvious, it is surprising how many people think they have to go over the agent's head. In fact, most agents will be responsive to a complaint if it is courteously presented. After all, these people earn their living by negotiating. If they know anything, they know that no one wins an argument.

Chapter 2, Gypsies, Tramps and Thieves 47

If you don't get satisfaction by discussing it directly with the agent, then the next step is to take it up with the agent's broker. The best approach is to adopt the stance that the agent merely made a mistake. Don't use threats and intimidation — that just makes the broker determined to defend the agent. The best approach is to explain what happened calmly and why you are upset. It's best if you can give the broker a graceful way to admit you are right — something like "I'm sure this was just an oversight."

If push comes to shove, then there are two remaining avenues before talking to an attorney. If the agent is a Realtor®, you can contact the local board of Realtors®. Some boards will attempt a simple mediation via a phone call, which can sometimes be successful. As a consumer you have a right to file a formal complaint with the agent's local board and ask for a hearing. This is expensive, as you will be expected to pay an arbitration fee.

I might also add that almost all earnest money agreement forms (offers to purchase) contain a binding arbitration clause today. Before filing a suit, either party must go through the arbitration process. This is actually a good deal, as the cost of arbitration is considerably less than the cost of a lawsuit.

Of course, if the agent is not a Realtor®, then the local board has no jurisdiction. However, all licensees, even Realtors®, are under the thumbs of the state licensing agency. In Washington that is the Washington Real Estate Commission, which can be reached at 360-586-4602 in Olympia. In Oregon it is the Oregon Real Estate Agency, 503-378-4170. Both agencies have the legal authority to investigate wrongdoing by licensees, and to revoke or suspend their licenses. They do not, however, have the authority to enter a judgment against an agent for damages in your favor. For that you need an attorney and a court of law. Nevertheless, the threat that you might turn it over to the state licensing agency should be sufficient to get action.

Oh world! World! World! Thus is the poor agent despised.
SHAKESPEARE, TROILUS AND CRESSIDA

WELL, IF BEING 'REALTY MAN' HELPS YOU SELL HOUSES, CHAMBERS, THEN GO FOR IT...

Chapter 3

You'll Appreciate Appreciation

Question: When is the best time to buy real estate?
Answer: Any time in the past.

If you're just interested in shelter and don't view your home at least partially as an investment, then you can skip this chapter. But for most buyers, appreciation is at least part of the reason for buying a home. If that describes you, read on.

Ask real estate investors how to make a profit when selling real estate and they will tell you the time to think about selling is before you buy. Not all homes appreciate in value at the same rate. It makes sense, then, to buy a home that has the best chance of fast appreciation, all other factors being equal. Of course, no one's crystal ball is 100% accurate. Nevertheless, historical trends help you stack the odds in your favor.

Before getting into this any deeper, I should make a minor correction. As a technicality, real estate does not "appreciate" very much. It does increase in market value, but mostly due to the fact that the dollar goes down in value, not because the real estate itself increases in value. What appears to be an increase in value is really the effect of inflation. Technically, this is not appreciation. True *appreciation* is when the property increases faster than the inflation rate due to other factors — e.g., you bought land in the path of a rapidly expanding city. Inflation is something you can pretty well count on, but true appreciation is usually due to luck.

Either way, you win. But purists would like us to distinguish between the two causes of increasing property values. Keeping them separate in your mind does help you think about which property has the best chance of increasing in value. Nevertheless, I'll just use the term "appreciation" here, since only nitpickers would care about the difference between inflation and true appreciation.

Inflation is not a local issue. If the dollar goes down in value, it does so equally throughout the country. In this chapter you want to determine which specific property will have the highest appreciation rate. Since inflation affects all property equally, it is not something you have any control over.

Similarly, other national economic conditions affect the appreciation rate, but may also be something you cannot control. For example, real estate is very sensitive to interest rates. If interest rates go up, fewer people can afford to buy, and demand shrinks, causing a lowering of property values. The opposite is equally true — lowering interest rates bring about a real estate boom and rising prices. But again, interest rates affect all property equally, so they do not affect which house you should buy. Always remember that inflation and economic conditions are tides which affect all ships equally.

At the same time, there are numerous factors which create different appreciation rates for individual properties and can make a big difference in how much money you make on your home investment —

- Type of dwelling (house, condominium, etc.)
- Architectural style
- Condition
- Age of the structure
- How the property fits with the neighborhood
- Value of amenities
- Price range
- Lot size
- Location

These factors are independent of the inflation rate and economic conditions. As we shall see below, each item on the above list must be considered in relation to the others, not in isolation. When considering which property to buy, you have to weigh all the factors.

Type of dwelling

Let's start with the top of the list — type of dwelling. All other factors being equal, in my experience the regular house will outperform the condominium, which in turn will outperform the manufactured dwelling. (By "regular house" I mean a single-family, detached dwelling, sometimes called a "stick-built" house.)

There are exceptions, of course. For example, a regular house usually outperforms a condominium, but what if you are located in an area where there is unusually heavy demand for condominiums with an accompanying shortage of supply? Obviously, if this happens, then the condominium may outperform a regular house. But such market conditions would be highly unusual. Throughout the northwest (and especially in the metropolitan areas) government agencies have been promoting higher densities. To accomplish this they zone an abundance of land for multifamily use, at the expense of land for single-family dwellings. This drives down the cost of land for condominiums and encourages contractors to build them. The result is a slight oversupply of condominiums in relation to regular houses. This has been going on for many years, and there is little likelihood that it will change.

Of the three choices, manufactured dwellings are usually the worst in terms of appreciation. Not that there is anything inherently wrong with manufactured dwellings, but (again) available land skews the economics. Manufactured dwellings can appreciate some when located in certain rural areas. This is because there is usually abundant land, so space rental or land payments are low. In urban areas the zoning is too restrictive, so lack of land drives up space rental. In metropolitan areas there are owners of manufactured dwellings paying $750 a month for a small space. When buyers compare this to the cost of the mortgage payments on a regular house, the manufactured dwelling can't compete. For resale purposes, the dwelling itself may actually lose market value. If you don't own the land, you can end up with no appreciation at all.

Even if you buy the land for your manufactured dwelling, usually all you get is the increase in value of the land. This is because the companies manufacturing these dwellings can ramp up production to meet demand. There will never be a shortage of dwellings.

What about duplexes, three-plexes and four-plexes? Or even larger investment properties? Some buyers assume that these are the way to go because that is what investors buy.

First, the woods are full of investors who have gone bankrupt, so following their lead is not necessarily wise. While some may be better educated in the world of business, there is no reason to assume they have any special intellectual gifts, and many obviously are working from the bottom of the brain trust. Furthermore, what makes you think investors don't buy single-family detached houses? The fact is, many do.

The reality is that, over the past several decades, single-family dwellings have averaged higher increases in value than multiple unit buildings in every area of the northwest. For example, in 1980 the median price of a four-plex in the metropolitan areas was approximately $96,000 and the median for a single-family dwelling was $63,000. Today the median prices in the same market areas are $215,000 and $160,000 respectively, or 223% vs. 254% of their 1980 values. Of course, no one can say such trends will continue, but from a historical perspective, the single-family house has the edge.

Bottom line: Stick with single-family detached dwellings unless you have no other choice or you have some compelling reason to choose otherwise.

Architectural style

Architectural style can affect appreciation rates, but probably the least of all the factors. Does a modern ranch style house go up in value faster than a turn of the century house, or vice-versa? On average they are usually in a dead heat. Of course, there are lots of architectural styles, and some may make a difference.

For example, most professionals will tell you that a house that is architecturally pleasing (regardless of age or style) will go up faster than a house with no street appeal. However, now we're talking about art. Art tends to defy any attempt to quantify it into dollars and cents. Most investors believe that attractive houses increase in market value faster, but would be hard pressed to prove it. How do you determine that a house is especially attractive? Unless you're the next Frank Lloyd Wright or have special training in architecture, this may not be easy.

Real estate agents refer to attractive properties as having "curb appeal." This brings up an interesting point about the way buyers think. People buy a house based on the exterior appearance. If you have already started looking at houses, I bet you're doing the same. You want to drive by first. If it looks nice from the street, then you want to make an appointment to see the inside, right? Think about this for a minute. Do you plan to live in the front yard? Will you have the television and your easy chair out there? Logically, is what it looks like from the street important? It's really silly, isn't it? And yet, every buyer I've ever worked with has been more concerned with appearance from the street than the interior.

Probably we all do that because of our need to impress others. We want our friends and neighbors to think highly of us. Never mind the fact that hardly any of us live in perfect houses, we still want our house to look like it jumped off the pages of *Ladies Home Journal*. A couple days after we move in, there will be dirty dishes in the sink and a month later the yard will have weeds. Nevertheless we think it has to look perfect or we won't buy it. The point is you can save a lot of money by being realistic. Instead of trying to buy a house that is in perfect condition, which will be priced at the top of the market, buy a house that looks like real people live there. It's going to look that way anyway, so why pay a premium for a house with a manicured yard?

At the same time, you want to find a property that has good architectural appeal. When the time comes to sell it, you can spiff it up cosmetically, but if it's architecturally a dog, there isn't much you can do with it.

Bottom line: Find a house that is in ordinary condition, but has pleasing lines and features. When you go to sell it you can easily polish it up and sell it at the top of the market.

Condition

Condition is a tricky issue when it comes to appreciation. Generally, a well-kept property will go up a little faster than a poorly maintained property, but not enough to get excited about.

There are, however, other factors that may make a property in poor condition the ideal purchase. For one thing, if you're handy and willing to spend the time and money on refurbishing the property, the poorly maintained property may be the best buy of all. To do this properly, start by buying it right. In my experience, few buyers understand how to figure what a fixer-upper is worth. Most end up paying too much. Professionals first figure out the value of the property as if it were in perfect condition. Then they subtract the cost of labor and materials necessary to bring it to that condition. The result is the present value of the property as it sits —

> Anticipated value when refurbished
> - Cost to refurbish (labor and materials)
> = Present value

Where most people go wrong is by grossly underestimating the cost of labor and materials, as well as how long it will take. The bathroom and kitchen are the areas most commonly misjudged. If you have any question about this at all, get help. Seek bids from contractors before making your offer. Better to be surprised before you buy than after.

I've also watched buyers make mistakes thinking they could convert a house to a duplex or larger. Even assuming the zoning permits it, doing so is not necessarily economically sound. The problem is that the house is invariably an older house and the resulting apartments are not generally attractive to tenants. It is easy to misjudge the amount of rent such units will bring, especially if compared to apartments in properties originally built as multi-family structures. Rental properties are valued primarily on the amount of rent they can command, so it's easy to overestimate what the finished conversion will be worth.

Bottom line: Condition is a major factor in the price of a property, but doesn't have much effect on the appreciation rate once you buy it. An exception is the fixer-upper, which can bring handsome returns if you buy it right.

Age of the structure

Historically, in the resale market, the older house is just as likely to outperform the newer house as the newer house is to outperform the older house. A ten-year old ranch usually appreciates as fast as a 1930's English bungalow, assuming each is equally attractive and other factors are the same.

However, new construction is a different matter. Newly built houses always sell at a premium. Part of the reason for this is cost of land, materials and labor, but the main reason is because the market for existing houses always seems to follow the new house market. The real estate market has always been this way, and it will probably always remain like this.

What this means is just this: If you buy new construction you will experience slightly less appreciation for the first few years than if you bought a used house of the same size and style. If you live in the new house for ten years or more, the difference in overall appreciation probably won't make much difference. If you sell in four or five years, you'll be better off if you bought an existing structure.

Bottom line: New construction appeals to a lot of buyers. The builder's model home is professionally decorated and looks more appealing than most existing homes. But most buyers should resist the urge to buy new construction because it usually sells at a premium and it's harder to negotiate a lower price. It takes more years of ownership to recover the initial high price you have to pay.

How the property fits with the neighborhood

How the property fits with the neighborhood is very important. One of the saddest things is to see an owner trying to sell a property that is overbuilt for the neighborhood. The key to success here is to buy the smallest house on the block.

Of course, this advice may be more or less relevant, depending on the neighborhood. What if the neighborhood has a mix of different sized houses? Then the style of the neighborhood is "mixed sizes." You're still better off if you stick with the average, but you have a little more room to vary without suffering loss from having an overbuilt house.

Another thing to shy away from is a house that is architecturally unusual for the area. A lone English-style house from the 40's in a sea of modern ranches and split levels will be hard to sell and will suffer in sales price as a result. It may be a great house, but it doesn't belong there.

A house in a neighborhood that is in transition is always to be avoided. This may be difficult to spot, as most neighborhoods change very slowly. If you see encroaching commercial properties in a neighborhood, this is usually a tip-off that the neighborhood is changing. It doesn't have to be commercial either. Sometimes an older residential neighborhood will be up-zoned to allow small multifamily structures. People start converting their older houses to duplexes, three-plexes and four-plexes. It still means the neighborhood is in transition, and is best avoided for long-term appreciation.

Another warning signal is a neighborhood where all the properties are poorly maintained. This is typical of areas in transition. Note that if one individual property is poorly maintained, it means nothing. It is a danger sign only if most houses in the area are in poor condition.

It is easy to assume here that the older neighborhoods would be in more danger from change than newer neighborhoods. This is not necessarily true. In any town there is usually an area where the "old money" lives. The houses here are not only larger, but nicely kept up. The neighborhood is as stable as it is possible for a neighborhood to be. At the same time the town may have an area of expensive new tract homes, priced about the same as the "old money" neighborhood. What if there is a future construction of an industrial plant, or an airport, or something else that would be obnoxious, close to the new neighborhood? You never know what the future will bring, but the older neighborhood is where the movers and shakers live. They have political power. Their neighborhood may be old, but it will probably be the least affected by future adverse changes.

I should also mention the problem of houses in commercial areas. As a general rule, stay away from this. You find houses all the time in areas that were solidly residential when they were built, but which are commercial today. As a rule, these properties do not appreciate as fast as houses in regular residential areas. Nevertheless, there are some reasons for buying such a property.

Suppose you find an attractive older house that has been rezoned commercial, probably along a busy street. If you have a commercial use for the house (i.e., you are self-employed and want to run a business there), then this may be an ideal property. It may not go up in value as fast as houses in a residential area, but that doesn't necessarily matter if you are getting a benefit from the property in the form of use for your business. After all, you wouldn't be allowed to run the business in a residential zone, so you would gain by saving all the money it would cost to maintain separate residence and business locations.

Bottom line: Buy a house that is average for the area or of lesser value than the average. Never buy the best house in the neighborhood as the lesser neighbors will hold it back. Never buy a property that is unusual for the neighborhood, whether as to size or style. Also look for proximity to adverse influences that could change the value in the future.

Value of amenities

Another thing to watch out for is a property that has a benefit that isn't really a benefit. Years ago I had a house listed that had a lovely, in-ground swimming pool. I'm sure it cost the owner at least $20,000 to have it put in. The house itself was an average ranch in a suburban area. I showed that house, held open houses, but had a devil of a time selling it. The interesting thing is what buyers said. At least half the buyers asked me if I knew how much it would cost to have the pool filled in.

The point is that, to the owners, the pool was worth what they paid for it. But to the average buyer, it was worth little or nothing. Real estate appraisers have a term for this. They would say the owners misapplied the principal of contribution. According to the principal of contribution, all components of the property contribute something to the overall value, but not necessarily in proportion to the cost, and sometimes even negatively. In other words, just because the owners paid a certain amount for some improvement, does not mean the property has increased in value by the amount of the expenditure.

This principle can get kind of interesting. In the example of the house I had listed, the pool added little or nothing to the value. The house was otherwise a nice house, of about 1,600 square feet. Now consider what would happen to the value of a $400,000 house if the owner spent $20,000 on installing a swimming pool of the same type. The owner would be much more likely to recover the cost because a pool fits with a house in that price range.

And the amount of the contribution can be greater than the cost. There is an old saying in real estate — "paint, properly applied, is worth $100 a gallon." In other words, a good paint job adds more value than its cost. Keep this in mind as you are shopping, and don't pay extra for things you can add inexpensively yourself later. And when you make improvements over the years, be careful to make sure they will increase the value by more than the amount of the cost.

A long time ago real estate agents were taught that properties on a corner were more desirable. In retail properties this has always been true. For a house, it has never been the case. A merchant wants as much sidewalk area as possible, but for a homeowner, being on a corner is a minor detriment. Most buyers look for as much privacy as possible. Being on a corner means your back yard is more exposed.

For some reason people in the real estate field got these two issues confused and it became "common knowledge" that being on a corner is always good. Don't believe it. It's not a huge disadvantage, but don't let anyone tell you it's a plus.

Even more important is the effect of a busy street. Single buyers are especially prone to assume it doesn't matter. If you're single you have no children, so you're right — to you it really doesn't matter too much — until you go to sell. Then you will discover that most buyers of single-family homes have children or plan on having them. The last thing they want is a house on a busy street.

Bottom line: Don't buy a property because has features that are attractive to you. Buy a property that has features that will be attractive to your buyer years down the road. Think about what most people want, not what you personally like. You can safely ignore whether a house is on a corner or not, but stay away from houses on a busy street.

Price

The price you pay for the property has a bearing on the percentage of appreciation, depending on economic conditions. Let us suppose, for example, that properties in your area go up in value by an average of, say, ten percent over a given period of time. That means that a $100,000 house will increase by $10,000 and a $300,000 house will increase by $30,000.

But the reality of the marketplace is usually weighted in favor of the lower-priced property, all other things being equal. Over the same period of time in a typical community, the $100,000 house may go up 20% while the $300,000 house goes up 10%. This is due to supply and demand of lower-priced housing. Builders make more money on larger houses, so the trend is for new houses to get larger and larger. This creates a shortage of homes at the introductory level.

However, in a recessionary period, the opposite holds true. When unemployment increases, the first buyers to leave the marketplace are the first-time homebuyers. People with more money tend to be more stable, so the market for higher-priced homes is not affected as quickly or as severely. Since most periods throughout history are expansionary, not recessionary, the odds are that you will do better percentage-wise with a lower-priced house than an expensive one.

Bottom line: Cheaper houses have gained in value at a higher percentage rate historically than more expensive ones. Of course you're a first-time buyer, so that's probably what you're looking at anyway. Still it's nice to know you're playing the odds right.

Lot size

The size of the lot can also influence the percentage of appreciation if it is unusually large or unusually small. In rural areas, land value has not increased as fast as the value of the improvements. Therefore, if the price you pay for the property includes a significant amount of land, you won't get as high an overall percentage of appreciation as if the property had a more ordinary sized lot. In urban areas, the opposite is usually true. The percentage increase in lot value for Portland and Seattle over the past ten years, for example, has outstripped the percentage increase in improvements. Twenty years ago in the cities the ratio of lot to improvements for a typical house was about 20/80 (20% of the value in the lot and 80% in the improvements). Today the ratio is closer to 35/65 (35% in the lot and 65% in the improvements).

Even in rural areas there is an exception if the property is in the path of growth, and that growth happens suddenly and quickly. This sort of event is the stuff of real estate legends — buying a property and reselling it a few months later for many times the purchase price because a big corporation wants the land for an industrial plant. In the real world, it doesn't happen. Nowadays properties are so tightly zoned that change of this nature is no longer possible. Getting a zone change is usually just too difficult for big companies to want to bother. If it does happen, it takes decades. Real estate is a solid, stable investment, not a way to get rich quick.

Bottom line: Buy a property with a lot size that is typical; neither smaller than similar homes in the area, nor larger.

Location

There is an old question in real estate —

Question: What are the three most important factors in real estate investing?

Answer: Location, location, location.

This is not really accurate, since we already know there are various other aspects that affect the appreciation rate besides location. Nevertheless, it underscores the fact that location is by far the most important factor in maximizing appreciation.

However, the beginner erroneously assumes that "location, location, location" means that you should buy in the most expensive area you can afford. This is not true. "Location, location, location" just means that location is an important consideration. The cheaper areas of town can have the highest appreciation rates as often as the most expensive.

Ask any group of property owners which part of town has the fastest appreciation. Those willing to venture a guess will usually pick their own neighborhood. Those who don't pick their own neighborhood will choose the most expensive neighborhood in town. Most people assume that properties in Snob Heights are good investments because that's where the rich live. And we all know the rich get richer and the poor get poorer, right?

All these people are right — and they're all wrong.

The fact is that *all* neighborhoods go up in value. Over the long haul, they will increase in value equally. In the short term, however, individual neighborhoods appreciate at different rates. For three or four years one neighborhood will be hot. Property values will increase twice as fast per year as the rest of the town. Everyone in the local real estate community will be aware that the neighborhood is hot. Investors will also figure it out. This drives demand, which just makes property values increase even more.

Eventually the bubble bursts. Except, unlike the stock market, real estate values don't skyrocket one day and plunge the next. Change is very slow, imperceptible from day to day, and even from month to month. Once the hot neighborhood has peaked, it will sit stagnant for five or ten years. There will be a modest annual increase, but usually a little less than the average for the town as a

Chapter 3, You'll Appreciate Appreciation

whole. The neighborhood is equalizing to make up for the period of hot price increases.

In the meantime, some other neighborhood will heat up. It will go through the same phases. In similar fashion, every neighborhood will do the same thing. Over the long haul, every neighborhood will have its day in the sun.

Is this important to you as a homebuyer? It depends on how long you plan to live in the house before moving on. Most first-time buyers think they're going to live in their new home forever. Yet statistically the average home sells between every six and seven years, so apparently most of them are wrong. Assuming you live in the house for six or seven years, buying in a neighborhood that is just starting to heat up can be an excellent way to cash in.

Now comes the problem. How do you identify a neighborhood that is about to take off? This requires research if you want to do it right. In small towns and rural areas, the data may not be available at all. In this case all you can do is talk to old-time investors and agents. Their gut feelings can be surprisingly accurate. In the larger towns and cities it's easier, as there are usually statistics available that will show you the percentage increase per year for different neighborhoods. In most cases your real estate agent can get the data for you from the multiple listing service. Just find a neighborhood that has had lower than average increases for the past five to ten years, and that is the neighborhood which is likely to pop next.

Bottom line: Don't buy in a neighborhood if everyone says it is hot. By the time everyone has heard that an area is hot, it's no longer hot. You want the *next* hot neighborhood. Use statistics to find it.

Now that we've covered the types of property, I should also make some mention of timing and market conditions. It is axiomatic that most people want to buy when economic conditions are generally hot, and few want to buy when we are in a recession. However, those who buy during a recession always make more money. The reason is very simple — when there are few buyers, sellers become much easier to deal with.

Investors know that to be successful you must be a contrarian. By a "contrarian" we mean you must buy when everyone else wants to sell, and sell when everyone else is buying.

The problem is that during a recession interest rates are always high — after all, high interest rates are the cause of a recession. And if interest rates are high, mortgage payments will also be high.

I recall selling real estate during the most serious recession we had in recent history — 1978 to 1982. I had no problem selling houses. If a buyer complained about the interest, I just said "if you don't buy now, what will rates be like next year?" The buyers believed it because everyone believed it, including me. We had never seen interest rates that high. There didn't seem to be any end to how high they would go.

The problem was not making the sale, but closing it. It seemed that every sale I made fell through because the buyers couldn't qualify for the financing. At the high interest rates of the day the monthly payments were too high to meet the lenders' qualifying ratios. I watched helplessly as sale after sale fell through.

What happened was that sellers had no choice but to carry contracts if they wanted to sell. And because there were not enough buyers, they lowered their prices to attract the few remaining ones. The interesting thing is that over the ensuing years most of those buyers made the highest profits I have ever seen home buyers make. The economic recovery of the late 80's increased demand for houses and prices went back up.

I have also seen markets that are overheated. Marketing time for new listings sometimes becomes a matter of hours. Buyers make offers above the listing price hoping to outbid other buyers. I can't tell you how many buyers I have known who got burned buying during such hysteria. My advice is to look elsewhere when things get this hot. Usually there is some other area of town that is not as frantic.

Bottom line: Don't be afraid to buy in a slow economy. Bad economic conditions spell opportunity for a buyer who is willing to bargain. But never allow yourself to get caught up in the buying frenzy of an overheated market.

Distressed properties

In the current real estate market, buying distressed properties is probably not going to work to your advantage, but it's always a popular subject so it deserves a bit of discussion.

First, a little terminology. In the real estate marketplace, the distressed property market is sometimes called the "REO market," which is a banking term from "real estate owned" — in other words, properties the lender owns because they have had to foreclose. ("REO Department" sounds much better than "Foreclosure Department, so that's what most lenders call it.)

There are several sources for REO properties. Lenders, of course, are the most obvious. But county tax departments frequently have foreclosures to sell, as does the IRS, the FHA, the federal Department of Veterans Affairs, state revenue departments, and various local government agencies. All have lists available. However, most sell through real estate agents, so your agent can automatically show you any of them the same as any other property.

The problem today is that you aren't going to get any good deals this way. Buyers are always convinced that there are government houses they can get for $10, but it just isn't so. Lenders and government agencies want to get as much as they can for the properties, so they always hold out for market value. In fact, in my experience, they get even more than market value because stupid buyers assume it must be a good deal and pay whatever the government is asking. The only time you can make money on foreclosures is during a period of severe economic recession and, even then, the good deals are few and far between.

It's pretty hard not to make money buying real estate. But by buying the right property at the right time you can make more than the average buyer. Of course, you also want a property that you are comfortable living in. No property is likely to combine the best features of potential for appreciation and still be the one you fall in love with. But that doesn't mean you should ignore the potential for appreciation.

According to a study by Chicago Title Insurance, the average buyer spends 4.4 months shopping for a home. While you are out there looking, keep the above points handy and apply them to the houses you look at. After a while it will become second nature to think about the appreciation potential of a house. Pretty soon you will be as savvy as the veteran investor.

The best investment on earth is earth.
LOUIS J. GLICKMAN

Chapter 4

The Art of the Deal

"Oh, you're in real estate? Great! I'm looking to buy a house. If you find a good deal, give me a call, OK?"

How many times I've heard that over the years! What I wanted to reply was "Forget it buster. If I find a deal like that it ain't gonna make it back to the office." Of course, I never said it, but I sure wanted to.

If a seller is desperate enough to sell at a bargain price, the listing real estate agent will buy the property on the spot. If the agent is too poor to buy it, someone else in the office will snap it up. One way or the other, it will never make it to the multiple listing service. I can guarantee you that you will never stumble across a real steal. Occasionally you can find a property that is fairly priced, but if you want a really good buy, you're going to have to make it one by negotiating. Good deals are made, not found.

That means you're going to have to learn how to bargain. Unfortunately, hardly anyone in our culture knows how to do that. We either pay the asking price, or we walk on by. When was the last time you dickered over the price of your groceries in the checkout line? Of course it isn't worth bothering to negotiate something like the price of a can of soup. But real estate is different. The stakes are high enough that it pays to learn how to bargain.

Getting preapproved

If Bill Gates has given you a signed, blank check, you can skip this step. If you're like the rest of us, though, determining your budget means finding out how much financing you can qualify for.

The next few chapters deal with loans in great detail, so I'll leave that subject until then. For now, suffice it to say that there are some less than reputable lenders out there. Use your agent to find one who will treat you squarely.

It's essential to get preapproved today. There is no way a seller is going to accept an offer without some indication that you can close the transaction. The stronger you look, the better bargaining position you are in. Lenders have reputations, like everyone else. You need to be preapproved by a lender known to be reputable by every agent in the community.

Don't settle for "prequalification" — you need full "preapproval." Preapproval means the lender has verified your income and credit history. The only thing remaining is the appraisal on the property. When you have been preapproved you can close within a couple of weeks. If you are merely prequalified, this means the lender still needs to do all the verifications. For further discussion of prequalifying vs. preapproval see the chapters on loan qualifying.

Let the shopping begin!

Now you're ready to start shopping. Assuming that your agent is acting as a buyer's agent, share your list of wants with him or her. Be as honest with your agent as you are with yourself. After all, you're on the same side. Remember, a buyer's agent must maintain your confidentiality. (If you're not using a buyer's agent, go to the chapter on agents and review the benefits.)

At this point the typical buyer goes into high-stress mode. Stop! It's just a house, for heaven's sake. Of course you're not going to do a perfect job of it the first time. But a hundred years from now no one will know that you made a couple of little mistakes, so cut yourself some slack and relax. As many years as I've been buying and selling real estate, I almost always make a mistake or two in every transaction. Stop trying to be a perfectionist.

Don't start by running around scouring the for sale ads scared you're going to miss something. Finding houses that fit your needs is your agent's job. You'll drive yourself nuts and your agent with you. After all, what's the rush? Unless your current address is an empty refrigerator box under a bridge, there's no urgency, so take your time.

Property values

Negotiating starts with comparing houses in the marketplace. You can't even know what kind of offer to make unless you know what the property is worth. That means the first step is to educate yourself about property values.

You don't need to become a professional appraiser to do this. In fact, although appraisers like to make up a fancy report with lots of big words, what they do boils down to comparing one property with others — the same thing that you can do for yourself. Nevertheless, a few pointers about appraising a property are in order.

The first thing to know about appraising is that it is an art, not a science. Any honest appraiser will tell you that getting an appraisal to within 5% of what the property will eventually sell for is the best they can do. Any closer is just dumb luck. The reason for this is because the properties are never identical and adjustments need to be made. Those adjustments are the appraiser's opinion, and therefore subject to error. For example, suppose the property being appraised does not have a fireplace, and the best comparable property does. Adjusting for how much extra the buyers of the house with the fireplace paid for it because it had a fireplace is difficult to do accurately. It's not like you can call the buyers up and ask them. And even if you could, they wouldn't be able to come up with an accurate figure either.

Another thing to bear in mind about property value is that there is no such thing as *the* value at any point in time. Value is not an absolute number; it is an matter of probability. If an appraiser says a house is worth $150,000, that means that there is perhaps a 75% probability that it will sell for a price between $147,500 and $152,500, a 90% probability that it will sell for a price between $135,000 and $165,000, and a 99% probability that it will sell for a price between $125,000 and $175,000. Appraisers usually appraise a property for the most probable selling price. That doesn't necessarily mean you are getting a good deal if you pay less, nor does it necessarily mean you are getting a bad deal if you pay more. The "appraised value" is just the selling price that is statistically the most probable, and that's all.

The comparative market analysis

A comparative market analysis (CMA) is similar to an appraisal, but with some important differences. (Occasionally you hear someone call it a "competitive market analysis," or "comparable market analysis," which I always figured were close enough not to bother arguing with them about it.)

One difference is that real estate agents cannot do appraisals without also getting an appraisers license, which practically none of them do. They can, however, do a CMA.

In some ways a CMA is like an "unofficial appraisal." It lacks the fancy language and, more importantly, it also lacks the price tag. Agents do CMAs for their clients for free. It's best not to abuse the service, as it does take the agent a bit of time to prepare one.

There is one significant difference between an appraisal and a CMA that you should bear in mind. Appraisals are almost always based on comparable properties that have sold recently, and that's all. CMAs, on the other hand, are based on comparable properties that have been sold, plus properties that are currently being offered for sale, and also properties whose listings expired unsold. The CMA format was originally devised by agents as a tool to help sellers figure out how to price their properties competitively. Therefore properties currently offered (the competition) and properties that expired unsold (probably because they were overpriced) are as important to the seller as properties that have sold.

When you get serious about a property, ask your agent to run a CMA on it and discuss it with you. The CMA format may have been originally designed for sellers, but it's just as valuable to buyers.

Distressed properties

Before getting into negotiation I want to take a minute and discuss the issue of distressed property. The term "distressed property" has always amused me. Let's face it, the property doesn't really care. It's the owners who are distressed.

But be that as it may, buyers always eagerly seek out distressed properties. In all the years I have been selling real estate, every buyer eventually asks me if I can find them a foreclosure, or a tax sale, or something they think they can get for ten cents on the dollar.

The reality is that it is just about impossible. There is an old adage — if it is too good to be true, it probably isn't. That applies here too. You have to ask yourself, why would anyone sell a property for less than it is worth? If a lender has foreclosed on a property and is now reselling it, why would they not ask full market value? Do you know any bankers who make a habit of giving things away? Ditto for sales of government owned property.

That having been said, there is one possibility. If you bid at foreclosure sales and outbid the lender, you can possibly get a bargain. This way the lender never gets the property.

There are numerous problems with this approach, however. First, in today's market, there are practically no foreclosure sales going on. Remember, the economy is good. People are employed. Defaults are rare today.

Second, even during bad economic times, the only time a borrower defaults is when the amount owing is more than the property is worth. In other words, worsening economic conditions have caused the property to go down in value to a point less than the amount of the loan against it. If the borrowers had any real equity in the property, don't you think they would have sold it sometime before the bank's foreclosure was final? Why would borrowers walk away and let the bank take the equity they had in the property? The fact is, the banks lose money on virtually every foreclosure.

And third, although there are rare occasions when you can make a good deal buying distressed property, it is a market that you have to follow carefully. You can't just walk in and pick up a good deal. You have to study the sales, follow the public notices, and make a complete business out of it. And when you do, you will be competing at the auction sales with other investors who work in this market. Your chances of getting a good deal are between slim and none. There is a far greater likelihood that your inexperience in this market will cause you to make an expensive mistake.

Bottom line: Forget the foreclosure and distressed property market today. Even during bad economic times, play this market only if you plan to be serious and follow it carefully.

Negotiation

The fundamental principle of negotiation is "he who cares least, wins." That's so important, I'm going to repeat it in really fat print here so you won't forget it —

He who cares least, wins.

If you never learn anything else about negotiating, learn that.

What does this mean when buying a house? It means that you can't care whether the seller accepts your offer or not.

A number of years ago I got a call from a local agent about a property she said was for sale. She was acting as the sellers' agent, but she said the sellers were "motivated." Among agents this kind of translates into "The sellers are really getting discouraged." As a listing agent she can't tell me what the sellers will do, but it's OK for her to fish for an offer when it doesn't appear the buyer is interested at the listed price.

The property had been appraised by the Federal Housing Administration (FHA) for $95,000 and the sellers had listed it at that price. After a couple of months with no offers, they lowered the price to $85,000. A couple of months later they lowered it to $79,000. This was when the agent called me.

I looked at the house and it was hate at first sight. The ridge line of the roof was sagging, the siding was uneven, the plaster on the inside walls looked as though it had been patted on by hand — it had been built shortly after the turn of the century, but whoever built it was obviously an amateur. The house had no redeeming architectural features. I couldn't even think of anything I could do to make it more attractive, short of calling in a bulldozer. The owners had already moved out, and had tried to spruce it up by having it freshly painted in and out, but it was still a dog.

I told the agent I hated it and had no interest in owning it. She insisted that the sellers were ready for an offer. I resisted. She kept after me for a couple of days. I wasn't just being coy with her — I truly hated the place. Finally I blurted out "OK, $40,000, and I hope they don't take it." She was taken aback, but the law requires her to write up and present any offer, so she had no choice but to take my offer to the sellers.

It turns out the sellers hated it even more than I did. They signed the contract without even a counteroffer.

Now, I should hasten to add that the deal I made wasn't quite as sweet as it sounds. In fact, the FHA had probably grossly overappraised the place. Not only was it not worth $95,000, it probably wasn't even worth $85,000. After all, the test of value is the marketplace. It had been offered for $85,000 for a couple of months with no takers, so it probably wasn't worth even that much. I suspect the real market value was somewhere around $70,000 to 75,000, still way more than the $40,000 I paid.

But now there is a problem. Typical first-time homebuyers go out, find a house, fall in love with it, and get so starry-eyed they sign whatever contract the agent shoves in front of them. If you fall in love with the place, you violate the fundamental principle of successful negotiation. *If you care more than the seller, who do you think is going to win?*

How do you get around this? After all, you don't want to live in a house you hate. The example I used above was for a house I was buying as an investment. I never planned to live in it, so it didn't matter to me how ugly it was. Its lack of style was relevant to me only when considering how I would sell it someday. I knew that, regardless of my opinion of it, there would be someone else for whom it would be a castle.

The answer is your agent. Your agent will be presenting your offer to the sellers, not you. If you were there in person, it would be hard to convince the sellers that you didn't care if they took your offer or not. Most of us aren't very good liars. And besides, it can easily come across as arrogance, which can turn the sellers against you. Your agent, however, can present it dispassionately. The trick is to keep your agent from knowing how much you care about the property. If your agent thinks your opinion of the house is so-so, that will be transmitted to the sellers, even if your agent says nothing specifically. They will read it in your agent's eyes, guaranteed.

And that brings me to an important side issue — never lie. Never ever lie. Not to your agent, not to the seller, not to anyone. Once you are caught in a lie (and if you lie, you will be found out, trust me), your credibility is shot forever. Successful negotiation depends on credibility, and that means telling the truth. Note that you don't have to spill your guts and disclose everything, just be sure that what you do say is the truth.

Not only must you never lie, but you must be genuine. The secret of success in negotiation is to act and sound reasonable and legitimate. If you come across as a slick high-roller, it will backfire, guaranteed. The best approach is to *act* as an amateur, but not *be* an amateur. If the sellers think they are facing a professional their guard will go up instinctively. You don't need them to be on the defensive.

Sales jargon

Before getting into negotiation techniques, it will be helpful if you understand a bit about the language of sales. Real estate agents like to consider themselves professionals, but at the same time they are salespersons. Understanding some of the jargon will help you understand what is going on.

There are two parts to every sale: The *pitch* and the *close*. The pitch is explaining about the product, extolling its features, showing it to the customer and presenting it in its best light. For the sale of a house, the pitch is showing the property.

The close starts when the salesperson asks for the order. Knowing when to stop pitching and close is kind of an art. If the salesperson asks for the order too soon, the buyer will not be ready to make the commitment. It's also possible for the salesperson to keep on pitching and forget to close. I've seen beginning salespersons talk themselves into a sale and right out the other side.

In selling a house, the pitch boils down to showing the property. The close is when the agent starts asking if you want to buy it. Usually the agent will start closing by trying first a trial close — like asking you if you would like to discuss financing options for the property. It's a little less abrupt than just asking "OK, do you want to buy it?" The agent figures if you are interested in discussing the financing, then you are sufficiently interested that you are ready for the final close.

Of course, if you're taking my advice in this book, you will have your own buyer's agent. In theory your agent should be pitching and closing on the seller, not on you. In reality, agents are so accustomed to pitching property to buyers that you can expect your agent to act a little like a sellers' agent in this regard.

He who is asking the questions is in control

One of the first things real estate agents learn is how to control the conversation. If you want the buyer or the seller to do as you want, you have to steer them in the right direction. Look at the following typical dialog when a buyer calls an agent about a house advertised in the paper —

"Hello, Aardvark Realty, how may I help you?"

"I'm calling about this cape cod you have in today's paper."

"Yes, that's a lovely home in the Fairhaven area. Is that an area that would interest you?"

"Yes, we have considered that area."

"This home has three bedrooms, would that be adequate for your needs?"

Notice what is happening here. When the buyer asks a question, the agent answers it and then follows it immediately with a question. Who is in control of this conversation? The agent can get answers to all his or her questions, while giving the buyer little or nothing in return. The agent will continue like this, extracting from the buyer how much they have for a down payment, how soon they plan to buy, and anything else necessary to determine if this is a serious buyer or just a tire-kicker. If the buyer is serious, the agent will go for the name and phone number and an appointment to meet.

I'm not saying it's not OK to answer questions. Sometimes it's fine to follow someone else's lead — if they're headed in the direction you want to go anyway. Just be aware that you are being a follower, and do so because you choose to do so, not because you weren't aware you were being manipulated.

Negotiation techniques

Most people can accept the principle that he who cares least, wins, but still feel uncomfortable making an offer below the asking price. Psychologists would explain this by pointing out that the fear of rejection is far stronger than the desire to gain. Most people will do anything to avoid rejection, including foregoing gain.

Get over this! A "no" is just a "no." They have not taken any swings at your personal being. Your mother still loves you. I know of no religion where it is a sin to offer less. In fact, I had a church buy a property I had listed once, and you would be shocked at the low-ball offer the elders started with. Smart negotiators know that offers and counteroffers are neither fair nor unfair. They are just negotiating positions. It's OK to offer less than the sellers are asking. Trust me on this.

Besides, you have to give the sellers the opportunity to say no. They might say yes, after all. Think of it this way — if you don't give the sellers the opportunity to say no, then you have just said no to yourself. You have denied yourself the chance to buy it at less than they are asking.

And remember, sellers expect the buyer to start out offering less than they're asking. Why not give them what they expect? Of course, there are limits — I've been in transactions where I felt that bringing the buyer and seller together would make bringing peace to the middle east trivial in comparison. Still, I've presented hundreds, if not thousands of offers. So far I've never had anyone take a shot at me because of the offer.

At the same time that you have to muster the courage to offer what you want, you must be careful not to come across as combative. There are two basic kinds of negotiators — those who view the negotiation as a battle to be won, and those who seek cooperation. In a slow market sellers will do business with combative negotiators because they have no choice. When they don't have to, they won't. As long as the economy remains strong, sellers can find adequate buyers without having to deal with jerks. Therefore, you have to make your offer in such a way that it appears you genuinely feel your offer represents what the property is worth. As long as the sellers think you are legitimate, they will consider your viewpoint as simply an honest disagreement with their viewpoint. If they think you are trying to steal the property, they will show you and your agent the door.

What this means is that you should generally avoid making low-ball offers. Offers that are significantly below the asking price are likely to evoke a negative reaction. If the sellers are asking $150,000 and you offer $100,000, not only will the sellers not take your offer, odds are they won't even make you a counteroffer. If you offer $135,000 you have a much better chance of getting at least a counteroffer.

On the other hand, there are exceptions to every rule. What if the property is grossly overpriced and has been on the market for a long time? This is a red flag already, because it means the sellers are probably not motivated. But if you want to test how much they want to sell, it would be an acceptable tactic to offer at market value or slightly less, provided you and your agent back it up with a CMA.

Negotiation strategies

There are so many successful negotiation strategies that this book would run to several volumes if I included them all. Since I can't cover all the possibilities, I will limit it to some common approaches. In the final analysis, your agent will have to tailor the exact strategies to the circumstances. Although you won't use all of them in any one transaction, here are a few strategies to give you some ideas —

• Buy a property that has been on the market a long time. One of the most common mistakes buyers make is thinking that they have to rush out every day and check the local paper to make sure they don't miss any new listings. This is the exact opposite of what they should be doing. Put yourself in a seller's shoes. You list your property and immediately a buyer makes an offer below your asking price. Would you take it? Not a chance. You'd want to wait and see if a better offer came along. To find realistic sellers you want only seasoned listings.

On the other hand, what if you'd been trying for months to sell the place. You've had no or few offers so far. Finally an offer comes in. There is a much better chance you'd say "to heck with it" and just take it. The longer the property has been on the market, the more humble the sellers become.

• It's best to wait 24 hours after seeing a house, then look at it a second time before making an offer. I guarantee that you will see a completely different house the second time around. If possible, see it once at night and again in the daytime. Realtors® hate this, but who's the boss?

• Offer a substantial amount of earnest money, in the form of a personal check. A personal check says "I am financially solid. I can write a personal check for a large amount of money." While any amount of earnest money is adequate to make the contract legal, you want to look solid, like you mean business. If the seller accepts your offer, you're going to spend it at closing in a month or so anyway, so any lost interest is trivial. It will pay much more handsome dividends if it sways the seller to take your offer. And if the seller doesn't accept your offer, the agent is required by law to return it immediately.

SIDE NOTE: The laws regarding clients' funds are strict. An agent must deposit all funds into a special "clients' trust account," subject to auditing by the state. The agent has three banking days to make the deposit in Oregon and one banking day in Washington. In both states, the agent can simply return your check to you without depositing it if the offer is presented and rejected before the time limit arrives. Once deposited, the agent may retain the funds for a reasonable time to be sure your check clears, but if your offer is not accepted, must return the funds promptly. Violating any of these provisions is one of the fastest ways to lose a license, and every agent knows it. Because of strict enforcement, you can give funds to a real estate agent with great confidence.

• Make your offer in writing. Verbal agreements involving real estate are not legally enforceable. And even if they were, they are unimpressive. Never forget what Samuel Goldwyn said — "a verbal offer isn't worth the paper it's written on."

• In most cases your agent should prepare a CMA and have it available when presenting your offer. Your agent should be prepared to go over the CMA with the sellers as a means of convincing them that your offer is reasonable. There are exceptions, depending on the nature of the property, the kinds of properties that appear from the database when the agent prepares the CMA, and the nature of your offer. Discuss with your agent whether taking a CMA to the presentation will help your cause or not. It usually does.

SIDE NOTE: In Oregon the listing agent may not prepare a CMA for a buyer that leads to the conclusion that the property is worth less than the listed price. This is because the license law does not allow the listing agent to offer the property at less than the listed price, and preparing a CMA for a buyer showing a value less than the listed price would be construed as suggesting to a buyer that it is not worth what it is listed for. A buyer's agent (your agent), on the other hand, is free to prepare a CMA for you regardless of what value conclusion it leads to, and may also discuss this CMA with the seller. Washington has no rule specifically on the issue of the CMA, but listing agents and dual agents there are also not allowed to offer the property at less than the listed price.

- Use the "alternative property tactic." It's called the alternative property tactic because your agent tells the seller "my client has another property they are also interested in, and if you don't wish to accept this offer they will surely want to offer on the other property before considering a counteroffer." This puts a lot of pressure on the seller to give your offer serious consideration.

Of course, there really has to be a second property, and your agent has to be convinced you are also interested in it. This is not difficult to do. When you are finished shopping you usually have a number one choice, a number two choice, etc. Just be sure your agent is aware that you have a second choice and be sure your agent plans to communicate that fact to the seller.

- Sometimes it's best to give the seller a very short period of time to consider your offer. Usually this works best when coupled with the alternative property tactic. Sellers' agents generally assume they can ignore your time limit. They figure you want the house, so you will still honor the sellers' acceptance even if it comes after your time limit. This is why you must make the sellers and their agent aware that they may not have a second chance to sell it to you.
- The "choice" strategy works by giving the sellers an option designed to camouflage what you are really offering. For example, suppose you offer to buy the house for $127,000 if the sellers will leave the range and refrigerator, or $125,000 without them. The sellers will quickly conclude that you are offering $2,000 for the range and refrigerator. Most peoples' used ranges and refrigerators aren't worth $2,000, and they probably know it. Eager to get $2,000 for their range and refrigerator, they accept the offer. What they really did was sell the range and refrigerator for $2,000, and throw in the house for $125,000. If the house was worth more than $125,000, you won. This strategy works by diverting their attention from the real object of the negotiation.
- If another buyer shows up, bow out. When there are two or more buyers, there is no way you are going to keep it from turning into an auction. Getting into a bidding war is the last thing you want. Be wary here. Sellers and their agents have been known to claim that there is another buyer when there really isn't one. Either way, you win by bowing out. If there is really no other buyer, they'll have to consider your offer alone. If there is, you have avoided a bidding war.

This brings up an interesting point about agents cooperating on each other's listings. The listing agent has probably been advertising the property for some time before you make your offer. This may have yielded one or more buyers who are interested, but not sufficiently interested that the sellers' agent could get them to make an offer.

Suddenly your offer appears. Remember, the sellers' agent owes the sellers the duty to do his or her best. That means the sellers' agent has no choice but to call all those buyers and tell them there's an offer on the property they were interested in. Two offers are better for the sellers than one. Nothing increases the appetite like prohibition. The minute the other buyers think they can't have the house they won't be able to live without it. And the result is that, by the time your agent presents your offer, it is not at all unusual for the listing company to come up with one or more offers too. Whenever that happens, I always call the listing agent immediately and say "oh, well let me withdraw my offer so you will have a clear chance to get your offer accepted." They're disappointed they can't get a bidding war going, but there is nothing they can do but sputter "OK."

- Concede on a minor point to gain a major one — closing date, possession date, terms, personal property included or excluded with the property, etc. Once when I was acting as a buyer's agent I had a buyer offer $105,000 for a property listed at $115,000. When I went to the presentation I expected significant opposition. It turns out that the seller (an elderly lady of substantial net worth) was concerned about being able to remove a rose bush from the row of bushes along the driveway. She was beside herself about the rose bush because it had been a gift from her grandchildren, but it was winter and she couldn't remember which one it was without seeing it in bloom. I suggested that we simply make a counteroffer to my buyers giving her the right to remove one rose bush of her choosing any time within 12 months after closing. She was so relieved about the rose bush that the price of the house was a minor consideration in comparison.

- Humanize yourselves to the sellers. If my buyers were a young couple buying their first home, I used to love to show them the property when the sellers were home so the sellers would meet them, especially if the sellers were older. Old people think young people are cute. They love to think they're helping them out getting their first home. Yeah, it's sappy, but it works. Believe me. Besides, you're not going to be young and cute much longer. You might as well get some mileage out of it while you still can.

- Use contingencies where appropriate. Many times buyers want to present the sellers with an offer than anticipates everything. They spend hours checking every detail about the

Chapter 4, The Art of the Deal

property from the zoning to the condition of the title. Not only will this drive your agent up the wall, it makes it more likely that the sellers will sell the property to someone else while you're fooling around.

Instead, condition your offer on contingencies. Lawyers refer to them as "conditions," but the courts also recognize the term "contingencies" as a synonym. Anything that you need to be sure about can be stated as a contingency. Some contingencies are so common they are included in the fine print of preprinted earnest money agreements — e.g. your offer is subject to obtaining the financing stated in your offer. Other common contingencies include making the offer subject to approval of an attorney, an accountant, a relative, a spouse, or making it subject to inspections, verifications, and anything else that worries you. Get the offer accepted first, then deal with the contingencies. After all, why bother checking all this stuff out if you and the sellers can't reach agreement on the price anyway?

- Don't "nibble." Nibbling means making a deal, then trying to get an even better deal after the other side has agreed to your terms. Normally, nothing will annoy the seller faster than trying to get an even better deal after the seller has agreed to your price and terms. If you do, don't be surprised if the sellers' reaction is "to heck with it," and they refuse to have anything further to do with you. However, if you make a contingency regarding something reasonable — such as inspections by professionals, and the professional inspection reveals unexpected repairs — the sellers will not be upset with you if you revisit the price you offered in the light of the results of the inspection.

SIDE NOTE: Be sure the inspection is confidential and will be reported to you alone. It is customary in the northwest for the buyer to pay the cost of the inspection (typically $225 to $250 these days), so there is no reason you should not insist with the inspector that the report be confidential. This gives you the option of sharing the inspection with the sellers, or not.

The sellers or their agent will have to let the inspector into the premises. They will naturally be concerned and follow the inspector around as the inspector goes through the crawl space, the attic, etc. Even if the results of the inspection are relatively clean (and there is almost always something negative in the report), this gives you a bargaining chip that will not appear as nibbling. Even if the inspector says nothing to the sellers during the inspection, they will expect the worst. When you later tell them about a problem the inspector uncovered, it will sound worse to them than it is, even if you are completely factual about it. Of course, you must have a contingency regarding the inspection in your offer, otherwise you cannot use this as a later bargaining point.

Both buyers and sellers frequently have misconceptions about inspections. One is that people think it is insurance — that the inspector is obligated to repair any problems not disclosed in the inspection. This is not the case. The language of the inspection agreement you will sign with the inspector pretty much absolves them from any liability.

Another trap unwary consumers fall into is agreeing to an inspection from a company solely on the basis of the price they quote, without reading the fine print. What areas and components of the house will they inspect? If they exclude the furnace, the roof and the plumbing, what good is it?

It is also common to exclude inspecting for pest infestation. This can include termites and carpenter ants. Termites don't care a lot for the climate in the northwest, although you do find them now and again. Carpenter ants love it here, however, and can destroy a home just as fast as termites. Of all the destructive problems we have here the most common is dry rot. "Dry rot" is the stupidest term in the language, because it is caused when wood remains wet; the exact opposite of what it sounds like. Luckily dry rot is the least common inspection problem because it is usually readily visible. Just be sure your inspection agreement covers everything you think it needs to.

You are better off with an inspector who is a member of a professional organization which has a code of ethics and standards of practice. To find an inspector, see the Resources section at the back of this book.

- Be neutral with the sellers about what you think of the property. If the sellers are home when you view the property, don't say anything about the house one way or the other. If you gush about the wallpaper, the sellers will be flattered, but may also assume you've fallen in love with the place. On the other hand, if you are negative about the property you risk insulting the sellers. Best to say nothing. Of course, if the roof has fallen in, it may be necessary to acknowledge reality. Just don't paint it either positively or negatively.

- Be careful with low-ball offers. A low-ball offer will usually backfire. Most sellers will refuse even to make a counteroffer when presented with a low-ball offer. If you wish to make an offer that is seriously below the asking price, you have to justify it. A CMA showing the property to be worth what you are offering is imperative. And regardless of what you offer, make it a ragged amount. For example if the sellers are asking $129,950, offer $122,300, not $122,000 or $123,000. This makes it appear that you have given the price serious consideration and that is what you really think it is worth, to the penny. If you make it a round number it looks as if you are just testing the water.

- Patience wins the prize. If the sellers make you a counteroffer, sit on it. The longer you take, the more anxious they become. This is very hard to do, especially for beginners at the negotiating game. Nevertheless, you have no choice. The more quickly you respond, the more eager you appear. And the more the sellers think you want the house, the more they will hold out for.

- When offering and counteroffering, make your increases progressively smaller. Suppose you offer $122,300 on a property listed at $129,950. The sellers counter at $127,500. You make a new offer at $123,500, an increase of $1,200. They counter at $125,000. You then make a new offer of $123,800, an increase of only $300. This tells the sellers that you have an upper limit and you've reached it.

- Never make "take it or leave it" offers unless you really mean it. At some point you should cut off negotiating. Then it's appropriate to say "this is our final offer." If you later agree to make another offer, you blow your credibility. A final offer must be just that — a final offer. Be prepared to walk if they don't take it.

- Blame your inability to meet the seller's price on a third party. "I'd pay your asking price of $135,000, but my (insert third party here) thinks it's worth only $125,000." Many first time buyers find that shopping with their parents in the car is an excellent way to shift the blame to someone the sellers and their agent can't reach. It doesn't have to be the parents — a trusted friend, an older sibling —anyone will do. The third party can also be used just to delay the process in order to make the sellers more anxious. "We'd offer right now but our (insert third party here) wants us to look at another house first." Letting the third party take the heat can be an excellent negotiating ploy.

Instead of blaming your inability to negotiate on a third party, couples sometimes find it easier to blame it on each other. "I'd love to offer more, but my (husband/wife) won't let me." There isn't much the sellers can do here. Decide beforehand who is going to be the heavy, of course. (OK, I admit it. I learned this technique from watching a cop show on TV. It's just an adaptation of the good cop/bad cop interrogation technique. But hey, it works!)

When you have made the deal

Once you have made the deal — offer made and accepted — you will immediately feel terrible. You will be consumed by self-doubt, depression and anxiety. "What have I done," you will cry to yourself.

This is called "buyer's remorse," and it happens every time. As many times as I have bought properties, I still have pangs of buyer's remorse with each new one. I just learned to shrug it off. You can trust me on this: Buyer's remorse is not fatal. I have never heard of it causing death or permanent damage. It may not go away until after you have moved into the house, but you *will* get over it eventually. And when you do, your lives will be much better than before. You'll be homeowners!

Always be on your guard, because you are one of the people who can be fooled some of the time.
ANONYMOUS

Chapter 5

Have I Got a Program for You!

There is so much to say about financing, I couldn't possibly get it all into a book this size. Even if I could, most people would find it dreadfully dull. Let's face it, financing isn't nearly as exciting as planning how you will decorate your new home.

Still, doing it wrong can cost you tens of thousands of dollars. You need at least some information to be sure you have an appropriate loan package and the right lender. But because there are so many variables involved in financing, you will have to rely on your agent and lender for the details. All I can do here is go over the basics of the different loan programs. When your agent or your lender recommends a specific kind of loan, at least you can look it up here so you'll know what he or she is talking about.

Before I get into the programs I want to give you a little historical perspective. What the various agencies do, what programs they have developed, and how they operate today is much easier to understand if you see how modern real estate financing developed.

In 1934 Congress enacted the National Housing Act, and created thereby the basis of all financing developed since. The National Housing Act established the Federal Housing Administration (FHA), whose sole purpose was to insure loans against default. Today, that purpose has not changed. If you borrow on an FHA loan and later default, the bank that lent you the money won't lose a dime. The FHA insurance will pay off the lender.

This was an incredible innovation in lending, an idea never

before conceived of. The motivation for creating insured loans was to encourage lenders to make real estate loans. After all, 1934 was the middle of the depression. The idea was that, if lenders would make loans for home buyers, this would stimulate demand for housing. Builders would be able to sell new homes, and thus hire workers to build them. Financing would start the economic chain — with adequate financing, buyers would buy; once buyers started buying, jobs would be created.

The National Housing Act was not without its opponents. The promoters of the plan suggested that the borrower be charged one half of one percent per annum as an insurance premium. Like any other insurance program, everyone's premiums would be pooled into a fund to pay for losses. Opponents said the amount of the premium was too low, that there would be so many defaults that the government would have to step in and bail out the fund.

In fact, what happened was one of the biggest success stories in the history of government. Except for a couple of years, every year since 1934 the FHA has made a profit. (Do you think we should turn the people running the FHA loose on the rest of the federal budget?)

The secondary mortgage market

But there was something even more important about to happen. Shortly after the creation of the FHA, banks started wanting to sell their FHA loans to investors. The idea of selling loans was not new — lenders have been dealing in paper since at least the time of the Romans, and probably even earlier. The problem was that creating an organized market for real estate loans was never possible because there were no standards.

The new FHA loans changed all that. Not only were the loans insured by an agency of the federal government, but FHA established minimum loan requirements. An investor buying an FHA loan was getting a known quantity. Banks were able to find investors to buy their FHA loans. The result was a greatly increased flow of investment capital into housing.

Within a few years banks needed to sell their loans at such a rate that it became necessary to expand the investor market. To facilitate this, in 1938 Congress amended the National Housing Act and created the Federal National Mortgage Association (FNMA). It didn't take lenders and investors long to change "Federal National Mortgage Association" to "Fannie Mae." A few years ago FNMA decided to recognize "Fannie Mae" as their official name.

Fannie Mae became the first in a series of new investment organizations developed to buy loans. We call Fannie Mae and the other investors who buy loans "secondary lenders." The lender who originates the loan is called the "primary lender." You won't personally have anything to do with the secondary lender. Your loan application, approval, and all the paperwork will go through your local primary lender. But rest assured that, sometimes within hours of making your loan, it will be sold in the secondary market.

Residential loans today are originated by various kinds of lenders — banks, savings and loans, mortgage bankers, and a few others. Every one of them sells all their loans in the secondary market. The big secondary lenders call the tune. If the loan doesn't conform to what secondary lenders want, the primary lender won't make it because there would be no one to sell it to. Luckily the secondary market is sufficiently diverse today that there is a market for almost any reasonable kind of loan.

Servicing

Secondary lenders are generally huge organizations with thousands and thousands of investors and hundreds of thousands of loans. Fannie Mae, because it is the oldest, is by far the largest. Its stock is traded on the New York Stock Exchange. The sheer size of secondary lenders creates a problem. Once they have bought the loan, they are entitled to all the principal and interest for the remainder of the loan. But how are they going to administer the millions of loans they own, covering homes all over the country?

The answer is that they don't. They leave that task to the primary lender. You will make your payments to the lender who originated the loan, who in turn will send them on to the secondary lender they sold your loan to. If you have a problem, you call your primary lender and they handle it — right up to foreclosing on behalf of the secondary lender, if necessary.

You may be wondering why primary lenders exist at all any more. If all the interest earned on the loan goes to the secondary lender, what's in it for the primary lender? Isn't that how lenders make their money — the interest?

The answer is twofold. The primary lender charges the borrower a loan origination fee. This fee is theirs to keep. And they charge the secondary lender a "servicing fee" over the life of the loan. Taken together, the origination fees and servicing fees ensure the profitability of the primary lender. It's a two-way street — the primary lenders need the secondary lenders to sell their loans to, and the secondary lenders need the primary lenders as their local agents to originate new loans and service existing ones.

In some cases primary lenders have found it advantageous to sell their servicing contracts to other primary lenders. The secondary lender doesn't really care who collects the money, just so someone does it. But selling servicing contracts has occasionally created problems for borrowers.

Once I had a loan on a rental house with a local savings and loan. Every month I would mail off my payment faithfully. Suddenly one day I got a past due notice from a lender I had never heard of. The notice indicated that the loan was already two payments past due. But it didn't indicate the property address, payment amount, or any other way for me to figure out what it was all about. I called the telephone number on the notice, but had to leave voicemail because the person handling this account was out of the office.

I put the matter out of my mind. I knew all my loans were current, so it was obviously just some mix-up that would get sorted out in due course. The person I left the message for never called me back, so I assumed they had probably figured it out themselves.

A couple months later I got a serious letter from an attorney representing the lender. It said that they were demanding that I pay the loan off in full within ten days or they would start foreclosure proceedings. But this letter had the property address on it, so now I knew it was one of my properties.

I hastily called the attorney and said I had canceled checks for all the payments and if he started foreclosure he would be facing a serious countersuit. He arrogantly told me he was sure his client was right and there was no way he was going to be "bluffed into calling off the foreclosure."

At that point I got out my check statements and looked at the canceled checks. They were right there — every one of them. Of course, they had been made out to and processed by the lender I had borrowed the money from. To make a long story short, the bank I had borrowed the money from had sold the servicing contract to the new lender. But they failed to notify me that they had done so. (When I complained they said "but there was a notice posted in our lobby, didn't you see it?")

Not only had they failed to notify me, but they continued to take my checks for payments on a loan they weren't even servicing any more! And sure enough, upon investigation, all my payments were sitting in a special account they had created because the bookkeeping department didn't know what else to do with them. Instead of sending them on to the new lender or returning them to me, they had just sat on them.

My problem, it turns out, was not unique. A lot of borrowers went through the same thing. As a result there are federal regulations requiring lenders to notify borrowers properly when servicing contracts are sold. And when you borrow money, the lender is required to give you a disclosure that they have the option to sell the servicing contract.

Mortgage brokers

Twenty years ago when you went to borrow money to buy real estate you dealt with a lender who had no branches outside of your state. Federal regulations did not allow lenders to make loans outside of their home state. Real estate lenders are now allowed to make loans anywhere in the country, which has created some interesting developments.

How does a lender make a loan in the northwest, when the lender has no offices here? The answer is mortgage brokers. Just as real estate brokers bring buyers and sellers together, mortgage brokers bring borrowers and lenders together. And just as real estate brokers charge a fee for their services, mortgage brokers charge also.

In traditional lending, a lender considered that the loan origination fee should cover the costs of originating the loan — that is, the salary of the loan officer and overhead associated therewith. But if a lender is not going to maintain an office and staff in the northwest, then the lender can use the loan origination fee as a commission to a mortgage broker who originates the loan.

The result is a mushrooming of mortgage brokerage companies all over the country. In a way, this is good. Mortgage brokers are paid nowadays on a strictly commission basis. If they don't originate any loans, they get no paycheck. This makes the mortgage broker the borrower's ally in getting the loan approved.

There is another advantage too — a mortgage broker can represent many different lenders. If you go to a bank, savings and loan or mortgage banker, the only loans the loan officer can make are the ones that lender does. A mortgage broker, however, may represent ten or twenty different banks, and an equal number of savings and loans and mortgage bankers. If one doesn't offer the specific program that is best for you, they probably represent another that does.

Unfortunately, there is a dark side to this development. Neither Oregon nor Washington requires a license or regulation of any sort for mortgage brokers who are engaged in loans to be originated by an institutional lender. (Licenses are required if a mortgage broker is going to sell loans to the public, but not if the loans are arranged for a bank, savings and loan, mortgage banker, or secondary lender.)

Without regulation, abuses have become rampant. Borrowers are getting fleeced right and left. You might think that the lenders on whose behalf the mortgage brokers are arranging the loans would step in and do something, but their efforts so far have been inadequate. As soon as the lenders prohibit a certain practice, the mortgage brokers figure out a way around it.

Now, obviously the vast majority of mortgage brokers are reputable and honest. It is probably only a tiny percentage that is preying on unsuspecting borrowers. Nevertheless, you have to be extremely careful. Make sure your real estate agent is aware of the problem and can steer you to a good lender. For further detail on the kinds of practices to avoid, see the chapter on predatory lenders.

Terminology

Before getting into specifics, a little vocabulary drill would make things clearer for you. Here is a brief glossary of lending terms that will help —

- Adjustment period — On an adjustable rate mortgage, how often the lender can increase/decrease the interest rate.
- Annual cap — The maximum interest rate increase that a lender of an ARM loan can impose in any one year. See also "lifetime cap."
- ARM — "Adjustable rate mortgage." A loan where the interest rate can increase according to some specified index.
- Balloon payment — A payoff required by the loan terms before the loan would ordinarily be paid off. For example, a 30-year loan could have a balloon payment requiring it to be paid in full at the end of seven years. Sometimes also called a "call feature."
- Conversion privilege — The borrower's right to convert an ARM loan to a fixed rate loan. To exercise the privilege the borrower generally has to agree to convert at the lender's current rate for fixed rate loans at the time of the conversion.
- Due on sale clause — Allows the lender to demand that you pay the loan in full if you sell the property. Usually also prohibits leasing for three or more years or a lease option.
- Index — An interest rate that is published to which lenders can tie the interest on ARM loans. Typical indexes today include Cost of Funds rate and the various treasury bill rates.
- Lifetime cap — The maximum increase possible over the lifetime of an ARM loan. Nowadays the lifetime cap is usually 5-6%. See also "annual cap."
- Loan to value ratio — The loan amount as a percentage of the sales price. For example, an 80% loan is a loan of 80% of the sales price, or a loan to value ratio of 80%. The loan to value ratio is usually multiplied by the appraised value or sales price, whichever is lower. With FHA loans an allowance for closing costs can be added.
- Margin — In an ARM loan, the amount that is added to the index to find the rate to be charged. For example, a loan tied to the Cost of Funds Index plus a margin of 2%, will be charged inter-

est at 2% higher than whatever the Cost of Funds Index is during the period. The margin is a constant over the life of the loan. (Note: typical margins are about 2 to 2½% — if you are asked to pay a margin of 3% or more you may be swimming with the sharks.

• Negative amortization — When the payments are not sufficient to pay at least the interest on the loan, the difference is added to the principal balance. Over time you end up owing more than when you started.

• Nonconforming loan — A loan which does not meet Fannie Mae/Freddie Mac guidelines. Usually the problem is that it is higher than their maximum, but there could be any number of other incompatibilities. Nonconforming loans must be sold to alternative secondary investors, which drives the cost up.

• Payment cap — If the interest rate increase on an ARM loan causes the payment to go up too much, lenders have discovered that it can cause defaults. To overcome this, many loans contain a payment cap, which artificially sets the payment lower than the amount indicated by the interest rate. This causes negative amortization.

• Prepayment penalty — A provision in a mortgage loan which requires the borrower to pay a sum more than just the remaining principal if the loan is paid off before its scheduled term. Years ago all loans had prepayment penalties. Then they became very unpopular with borrowers, so lenders stopped including the clause. Nowadays you can get a slightly lower interest rate if you agree to a prepayment penalty. Government loans never have prepayment penalties.

• Rate lock — When you make loan application the lender will quote their current interest rate, but is under no obligation to close the loan at that rate. If you think rates are going to increase before closing you can pay extra for a rate lock. Warning — lenders give you a rate lock only for a stated period of time. Before paying for a rate lock, ask the lender what percentage of their loans close within the lock period. A rate lock that expires before you can use it is not worth anything at all.

• Teaser rate — An initial interest rate substantially below market in order to attract the borrower. More common on credit card loans today, but also occasionally found on real estate loans.

Chapter 5, Have I Got a Program for You! 95

Amortization and math

OK, math is scary for some of you. But this stuff is easy. It's really nothing more than addition, subtraction and multiplication. You can do anything in this section with a common pocket calculator. (For using real estate calculators, see the section I have included at the end of this book in Appendix B.)

"Amortization" just means the process of paying off a loan in installments. The opposite is a loan where you make no payments of principal until the end, at which point you pay it all off at once. These are sometimes called "interest only" loans. Business loans are frequently structured as interest only loans, but consumer loans are almost always amortized loans.

Let's take a loan of $100,000 at 8% for 30 years. The monthly payment of principal and interest for this loan is $733.76. (You can get this from the amortization chart in Appendix B.)

That means that you will make a monthly payment of $733.76. When you make the first payment, the lender will calculate the interest for the first month, which comes to $666.67 ($100,000 times .08, divided by 12 months, equals one month's interest of $666.67). The remainder of the payment will be subtracted from the principal ($100,000). This gives a breakdown like this —

Interest —	$666.67
Principal —	67.09
Total —	$733.76

In other words, you now owe $67.09 less than when you started. Congratulations! You now owe only $99,932.91! (All right, this isn't very exciting yet. But wait a few years and it will start to look really good.)

Now, when you make the same payment for the second month, the amount of interest decreases because you owe less money. To be specific, the lender will charge you only $666.22 in interest ($99,932.91 times .08, divided by 12 months, equals one month's interest of $666.22). This makes the principal gain a little higher — $67.54. The breakdown for the second payment is —

Interest —	$666.22
Principal —	67.55
Total —	$733.76

In other words, you now owe $67.55 less than you did after the first month's payment, and $134.64 less than when you started. Your new balance to start the third month is only $99,865.36.

Notice that the principal gain accelerates over the life of the loan. You can see that in the following chart for the first year of the above loan —

Mo.	Beg. Bal.	Payment	Interest	Principal	New Balance
1	$100,000.00	733.76	666.67	67.10	99,932.90
2	99,932.90	733.76	666.22	67.55	99,865.36
3	99,865.36	733.76	665.77	68.00	99,797.36
4	99,797.36	733.76	665.32	68.45	99,728.91
5	99,728.91	733.76	664.86	68.91	99,660.01
6	99,660.01	733.76	664.40	69.36	99,590.64
7	99,590.64	733.76	663.94	69.83	99,520.82
8	99,520.82	733.76	663.47	70.29	99,450.52
9	99,450.52	733.76	663.00	70.76	99,379.76
10	99,379.76	733.76	662.53	71.23	99,308.53
11	99,308.53	733.76	662.06	71.71	99,236.82
12	99,236.82	733.76	661.58	72.19	99,164.62
	Totals	$8,805.12	$7,969.82	$835.38	

Notice how the principal gain column increases each month while the interest paid column decreases. Kind of nice, isn't it?

Anyway, this is what we mean by "amortization" — the regular payoff of a loan in installments. I gave you above just the first twelve months, but if you have a computer you can fire up your favorite spreadsheet program and create an amortization chart for the full 30 years of a loan (360 months). Then you can see how the principal gain is low at the beginning, but at the end is almost the entire payment.

Loan discounts and buydowns

Back when the FHA was started in 1934 a new wrinkle was added to the world of residential financing. In an effort to make home ownership more affordable, the FHA set the maximum interest rate that lenders could charge on FHA loans. They deliberately set this rate a little below market.

Unfortunately, this meant that no lender wanted to make an FHA loan. After all, conventional loans with 20% or more down payment were considered just as safe as an insured FHA loan. Why settle for a below-market rate?

The solution was loan discounting. The lender would make the loan at the highest rate the FHA would allow, and ask the sellers of the house to pay a "loan discount" to make up the anticipated loss of interest. Actually, it should have been the buyers who paid the discount, since the buyers were the ones receiving the benefit of the below-market interest rate, but the FHA quickly made a rule that the buyers were prohibited from paying any part of the discount. The only ones left to pay it were the sellers. And this worked reasonably well — the discount wasn't too terrible, and the sellers were usually getting a big check at closing, so it was affordable for them.

Although interest rates on FHA loans have been allowed to float at market for a couple of decades now, it is still common to find loan discounts. A loan discount is simply to buy the interest rate down. And anyone can pay it today, including the borrower, even on FHA loans, although it is usually still paid by the sellers. The sellers' motivations are to encourage the buyer to buy the house.

A discount is used to buy the buyer's interest rate down for the entire life of the loan. It generally costs about 1½% of the loan balance to lower the interest by ¼ of 1%. If you wanted to buy it down by ½ of 1% instead of ¼ of 1%, it would cost twice as much, or about 3% discount. While this can be a significant sum for the seller, the effect on the buyer is much less dramatic. Lowering the interest rate from, say, 8% to 7¾% on a 30-year loan of $100,000 lowers the payment from $733.76 to $716.41 — a savings of only $17.35 a month. But it will cost the seller about $1,500 (1½% of the loan balance) to get the buyer this benefit.

Although loan discounts started with FHA loans, they are now found commonly on conventional loans as well. And along the way, there are new variants that have been spawned.

One variation on the theme is the buydown. In fact, it is the same as a discount, that is, a sum paid (usually by the sellers) to entice the lender to lower the buyer's interest rate. The difference is that the buydown buys the interest rate down only for the first few years of the loan. A typical buydown might be the "2-1" buydown, where the interest rate is lowered 2% the first year, 1% the second year, and nothing thereafter. A bank would charge twice the fee (3% of the loan balance) for the 2-1 buydown, but the effect on the buyer is much more dramatic. Instead of lowering the payments from $733.76 to $716.41 for the life of the loan, it lowers the payment to $599.55 the first year, to $665.30 the second year, and back to $733.76 thereafter.

While it would be nice to have the payments lowered for the whole life of the loan, it is at the beginning where the buyer needs the help, not later. Therefore, the buydown would appear to be more popular than the discount. The reality is, however, that lenders aren't overly fond of buydowns. A payment increase from $599.55 a month to $665.30 a month in one year is just short of an 11% increase. You'd think that a borrower would remember that the payment is going to increase dramatically the second year of the loan, but some seem to forget. This can cause what lenders call "payment shock." A payment shock that is not remedied can lead to a default. It's a lot safer for the lender if the loan is bought down a smaller amount, but equally over the life of the loan.

Loan discounts and buydown costs are expressed in terms of "points." A point is simply 1% of the loan balance. For a $100,000 loan, one point is $1,000; 2½ points is $2,500, and so on.

There is another dimension to the issue of discounts and buydowns — loan origination fees. Lenders have charged loan origination fees for decades. These are a direct contribution to profit and overhead. Loan fees are also stated as a percentage of the loan balance, the same as discounts. If the lender charges you a higher loan fee in exchange for a lower interest rate — guess what? That's a discount. It ends up in the same pocket. It doesn't make any difference if you call it a discount or a loan fee.

The next question is, should you go for a discount or a buydown? The answer is, probably not. Not because there is anything inherently wrong with the idea, but because of the way they are marketed. For example, today it is popular among lenders to offer "no-fee" loans. That is to say, they are giving up their "dis-

Chapter 5, Have I Got a Program for You!

count." Guess where they're getting the money to compensate for not charging fees. If you guessed "a higher interest rate," you got it right! Lenders have figured out that the average consumer would rather save a couple thousand dollars in fees up front, even if it costs them $10-20,000 in additional interest over the life of the loan. Borrowers probably wouldn't if they knew how much it's costing them in additional interest, but since they don't know how to calculate what they're getting, they buy the lender's "no-fee" loan and think they're getting a good deal.

So how do you figure out if a no-fee loan is a good idea? It's ridiculously simple. First, ask the lender what the payment is on the no-fee loan, and what the payment would be on the same loan with their usual fee. Since they are charging higher interest on the no-fee loan, the payment will be higher than for their regular loan. Now multiply each payment by 360 (assuming it is a 30-year loan). This is how much each loan will cost you over the life of the loan, including principal. The difference is how much more the no-fee loan will cost you in the end. Compare this figure to the amount of the fees you will be saving.

For example, in a recent ad, a local lender was offering no-fee loans at 8¼%, and loans with a 2% loan fee at 8%. For a loan of $100,000 the calculation would go like this —

	8% loan	8¼% loan
Payment	$733.64	$751.26
	× 360	× 360
Total	$264,110	$270,453

Difference ($270,453 - $264,110)	$6,343
Amount of 2% loan fee on $100,000 loan	$2,000

Which would you rather do? Save $2,000 up front but end up paying $6,343 more in interest as a result? The no-fee loan doesn't look so hot now, does it?

On the other hand, there is an additional consideration. What if you live in the house for only six years. Now the total interest you will pay will be much less because you multiply the payments by 72 months instead of 360 —

	8% loan	8¼% loan
Payment	$733.64	$751.26
	× 72	× 72
Total	$52,822	$54,091

Difference ($54,091 - $52,822)	$1,269
Amount of 2% loan fee on $100,000 loan	$2,000

This looks a lot better, doesn't it? It appears that the no-fee loan is a better deal if you live in the property for only six years, but a loser if you live there for the full 30 years. Only you can make this calculation, because you are the only one who can predict how long you will live in the house. At least now you know how to do the calculation so you can make a fair comparison.

Federal Housing Administration loans

Now that we have some basic ideas of the way lenders work and some vocabulary, we can get down to the major loan programs available today. The FHA is the granddaddy of all. In fact, over the years it has always been the pioneer. As soon as it figures out a new program, others copy it. Therefore the FHA would be a good place for us to start.

While anyone can get an FHA loan, most FHA borrowers are first-time homebuyers. This is because, traditionally, FHA loans have been the most liberal as to down payment and qualifying requirements. The tradeoff is the mortgage insurance premium, which makes them a bit more costly than other programs. Still, if it's the only way you can buy, it's worth the slight extra cost.

The basic FHA program is called "Section 203(B)." This is a reference to the place in the federal code where it is described (section 203, paragraph B). Although the FHA has many loan programs for all kinds of special purposes, the 203(B) program remains by far the most popular.

All FHA loans must be for owner-occupied property. Of course, you can move out after you buy the house, but you must have had the intention of living in it when you sign the loan documents. With a 203(B) loan you can buy a single-family house up to a fourplex. Loans under 203(B) are also available for manufactured dwellings. (There is a separate program for condominiums, however — see below.)

The maximum loan amount varies according to what county you are located in. For a single-family house, the basic maximum amount is $121,296, which applies to most counties in the northwest. For metropolitan Portland the maximum goes up to $170,362, and for the Seattle area, $219,849. As you can imagine, there are also northwest counties that are between these extremes. In addition, the basic amount goes up from $121,296 to $155,232 for a duplex, $187,632 for three units, and $233,184 for a fourplex. In the higher cost areas these amounts are also increased. Important note: The FHA changes the maximum loan amounts sometimes as often as every three or four months. *If the above amounts are less than you are planning to pay for a house, call a local lender to see if the amounts have been increased since this book was printed.*

A low down payment is one of the main benefits of FHA loans. Although the actual calculation is kind of complicated, it runs to approximately 97% of the acquisition cost. One nice feature of FHA loans is that you can add an estimated amount for closing costs to the purchase price before calculating the loan amount — i.e., you can borrow the majority of the closing costs.

Another benefit is that the FHA sets the maximum allowable amount for many of the expenses the borrower has to pay. In reality this doesn't save a huge amount, because lenders just make up for it some other way. For example, FHA sets the maximum loan origination fee at 1%. Most lenders charge 2% or more for their other loans, so when making an FHA loan, the lender just charges a little more interest, a bigger loan discount, or get the difference out of your pocket some other way. Still, it's nice to know that someone is at least trying to watch out for you.

And speaking of treating you right, with FHA loans you have a go-between in case you need some serious help dealing with a lender. No one likes to contemplate financial distress, but the fact is, it does happen. What if you're suddenly unemployed, the real estate market is poor, you can't sell the house easily, and the lender is breathing down your neck? Remember, in the event of a foreclosure, the FHA will have to pay off the bank. It's their nickel, not the bank's. The last thing the FHA wants is a foreclosure, so it's in their best interest to have the bank cut you a little slack. While the bank won't listen to you, they will likely pay attention to a call from the FHA.

Because you can finance most of the closing costs, and the closing costs are slightly less than for conventional loans anyway, FHA loans cost the borrower much less in total cash expense. There is no conventional loan program that can get you into a house with less cash out of pocket. If the amount of cash you have to work with is tight, FHA may be the best alternative.

Another popular FHA program is Section 251, which is the same as 203(B), except that the loans are adjustable interest rate loans (ARMS). In times of rising interest rates, ARMS become increasingly popular with borrowers.

In you are interested in rehabilitating a property, Section 203(K) may be what you need. These are basically the same as 203(B) loans, but allow you to finance the cost of rehabilitation in the same mortgage as the acquisition. Most conventional lending for such properties would be very difficult. First, you'd have to make a big down payment, because conventional lenders don't like substandard properties. Then you'd have to get short-term temporary financing for the rehabilitation. And finally, once the place was finished, you'd have to refinance again to pay off the short-term loans. Some conventional lenders do offer to finance the acquisition and rehabilitation expenses in one loan, but treat it as a construction loan — high interest rate, with a very short term — meaning you'd still have to refinance to get permanent financing.

When making a 203(K) loan a portion of the loan amount is used to pay the seller at closing. The remainder is held in escrow on your behalf. As you complete the work, the funds are disbursed. A disadvantage of 203(K) loans is that there is a lot more paperwork involved for the lender. As a result, loan costs are slightly higher than for regular FHA programs. Still, it's usually a lot cheaper than going conventional. Section 203(K) loans are worth the effort, but can be maddening in the paperwork unless you have a mortgage broker who is experienced with them. If you are going to get a 203(K) loan, I strongly urge you to find a mortgage lender who is very experienced and has closed a number of them.

Condominiums have a special FHA program — Section 234(C). This section is also used for rowhouses. The basic provisions are identical to 203(B) loans.

Unlike most conventional loans these days, FHA loans are fully assumable by a buyer if you want to sell the house. The buyer must qualify, but the lender cannot increase the interest rate. This can be a plus when you go to sell the house, especially if interest rates in the marketplace have gone up.

Nehemiah down payment assistance

Nehemiah Home Ownership 2000, Inc. has created a down payment and closing cost assistance program that has become very popular. The purpose of the program stems from FHA rules regarding borrower investment in the property. According to the rules, borrowers must make a minimum down payment of 3% of the purchase price plus allowable closing costs, although part of that can be in the form of a gift. The problem is that FHA allows gifts only from the borrower's family and certain other individuals, but not from the seller. The purpose behind the rule is to avoid having the seller increase the price of the house by the amount of the down payment, then giving the buyer a "gift" of the down payment. This would result in buyers potentially having no money of their own invested, a sure way to increase the default rate.

Nehemiah Home Ownership 2000, Inc. gets around this issue by acting as a go-between. As a charitable organization recognized by the IRS and by the FHA, it's legal for it to make the gift to the buyer under FHA rules. The seller, in turn, pays a fee of up to 4% of the sales price to Nehemiah Home Ownership 2000, Inc.

To qualify under the program, the buyer's income must be under the median income for the area served, the buyer must make a minimum investment of 1% in the property, and the loan must be an FHA loan made by a lender approved by Nehemiah Home Ownership 2000, Inc. The gift funds cannot be used to pay off the borrower's other debts or for interest rate buydowns, although it can be used for expenses of the acquisition, including closing costs, loan fees, etc., as well as toward the buyer's down payment. The buyer must also attend approved homeowner education classes. The property can be any property that FHA will normally insure a loan on.

Within the past year Fannie Mae has come out with "Flexible 97" loans which can be used with Nehemiah gifts as well. The Flexible 97 program is basically a 97% loan to value ratio conventional loan. Its disadvantage compared to FHA loans is that it is somewhat more difficult to qualify.

U.S. Department of Veterans Affairs (DVA)

If you're not a veteran, you can skip this section. (For married co-buyers, only one needs to be a veteran.) But if you're a veteran, home loans under the DVA are one of the best deals around, so read on!

Loans under the DVA are referred to by a variety of synonyms — "federal GI loans," "VA loans," "federal veterans loans," and so on. They're all the same thing, as the DVA has only one basic program. (Note to Oregon veterans — there is also a home loan program available under the Oregon Department of Veterans Affairs, which has nothing to do with the U.S. Department of Veterans Affairs. Details are covered below.)

Federal GI loans started right after World War II when Congress passed the Servicemen's Readjustment Act of 1945, now Title 38 of the U.S. Code. Like FHA loans, federal GI loans are made by lending institutions, not directly by the government. There is a major difference, however. With FHA loans the borrower has to pay an insurance premium to cover the loan against default. With federal GI loans, however, the loans are guaranteed by the DVA for free as a veteran's benefit. This makes them very attractive, if you can qualify.

Another nice thing about federal GI loans is that there is officially no down payment required by the DVA. Some lenders do require a down payment, and most will lend at a lower rate if there is a down payment, so you may want to consider the benefits of a down payment if you can afford it. But it's nice that you have the option of no down payment if you want to.

Although there is no premium charged, the DVA does charge a "funding fee." The DVA uses the funding fee to offset costs of the program, including funds to pay for losses. Personally I always just figured "funding fee" was a fancy way of saying "insurance premium" without having to admit what it really is. Nevertheless, the amount is considerably less than FHA charges for insurance on their loans. The funding fee is 2% of the loan balance if there is no down payment, 1½% if there is at least a 5% down payment, and 1¼% if there is at least a 10% down payment (¾ of 1% higher for reservists). The funding fee is waived for veterans with certain disabilities, and spouses of veterans who died in service or due to service-related injuries. There are other cases where the funding fee is different from the standard amount too. Regardless of the amount of the funding fee, it can be added to the loan amount, so you won't have to pay it up front.

Like the FHA, the DVA sets the maximum amounts lenders may charge for certain expenses. One weird feature of DVA loans is that the borrower is never allowed to pay any part of an escrow fee. Escrow and closing are discussed in a later chapter, but for now, suffice it to say that the services of an escrow are neutral between buyer and seller. The fee is traditionally split 50-50 between buyer and seller throughout the northwest. If you get a federal GI loan, the seller would have to pay all of the escrow fee, so this will save you a bit of money in some cases. Of course, in Washington, a lot of loans are closed in the offices of the lender rather than in escrows, so there may be no fee at all anyway. In Oregon almost all sales are closed in escrows.

To obtain a federal GI loan you will have to get a Certificate of Eligibility from the DVA. The easiest way to do this is usually to visit the local DVA office in Portland or Seattle. (See the Resources at the end of this book for the address and phone number.) Be sure to take with you your separation papers from the service.

Eligibility is kind of complicated, because it depends on the period of time in which you served. For example, only 90 days active duty is required for World War II veterans, but for Persian Gulf War veterans 181 days of active duty is required (or two years if not on active duty). The time period is even different sometimes for officers vs. enlisted veterans. And to top it all off, the time period is waived if you couldn't complete your tour of duty due to service-connected disability. I should also add that surviving spouses are also generally eligible but, again, the details are complicated. Frankly, the easiest way to determine whether you are eligible or not is to contact the DVA office closest to you. If possible, I recommend doing this as soon as you have decided that you are going to use your DVA entitlement, preferably before you even start looking at houses. If you're a veteran, I don't have to remind you how long it will take the government to do things. (Actually, in fairness, the DVA is usually pretty responsive. Still, there is no reason to wait to the last minute.)

Unlike the FHA, the DVA does not set a maximum loan amount. They do, however, set the maximum amount of the entitlement, which Congress changes from time to time. The current maximum entitlement is $50,750. Now, don't panic here! "Maximum entitlement" does not mean "maximum loan amount" — it means that is the maximum amount of the guaranty. In other words, if you default, and the lender loses money after foreclosing on the house, that is the maximum amount the DVA will pay to make up the loss.

Lenders generally like the top 25% of their loans insured against default. Even conventional lenders do this these days. A little math tells you that, at a loan of $203,000, the guaranty entitlement is exactly 25% of the loan amount (4 times $50,750 equals $203,000). Therefore, lenders will generally not lend over $203,000 on a federal GI loan.

Just in case you make an enormous income and can qualify for a bigger house than you can buy with $203,000, there are a few lenders around who make larger federal GI loans. To do so, they will require a down payment of 25% of the amount of the purchase price that exceeds $203,000.

I should also mention that the last time the entitlement was raised was October 13, 1994. If the entitlement should be increased (which could happen at any time), the maximum loan amount will go up correspondingly. Just remember that the maximum loan amount without a down payment is always four times the maximum entitlement.

You can use your entitlement to buy a house, or up to four units. You can also use it to buy a condominium, rowhouse or a manufactured dwelling. Regardless of what you buy, it must be owner occupied. Like FHA loan programs, this means you must have the intention to occupy the property when you sign the loan documents.

Like FHA loans (and unlike most conventional loans), DVA loans are fully assumable when you go to sell the house. Your buyer must qualify, but the lender cannot raise the interest rate because of the assumption. This can be a good thing if market interest rates have gone up.

You can also get your entitlement fully restored under certain circumstances. If you sell the house you can have it restored if your buyer is a veteran who uses his or her own entitlement, or if the loan is paid off in full. (But if you sell it to a non-veteran who assumes your loan, then your entitlement is not restored.) You can also reuse your entitlement in order to refinance your existing DVA loan later. This is especially nice if interest rates have gone down and you want to take advantage of the lower rates. You might also want to refinance if the property has gone up in value and you need the cash from the equity for some other purpose (such as starting your investment program in rental properties on the way to becoming a land baron).

The Oregon Department of Veterans Affairs (ODVA)

Washington people can skip this section. Only five states have state GI home loan programs, and Washington is not on the list. Oregon, however, was the first state to have a home loan program for veterans, and it has been very successful and popular in the past.

The basic idea of the ODVA home loan program rests on the fact that the federal government exempts interest income on state and local bonds from income taxes. Therefore, the state can sell bonds at interest rates well below market. The funds are then used to make loans to eligible veterans, again at below market interest rates. Note that these are direct loans — unlike FHA and DVA loans where a commercial lender makes the loan with government insurance or guaranty. Borrowers with an ODVA loan make their monthly payments directly to the Oregon Department of Veterans Affairs.

Getting a loan at below-market interest rates is a cool deal. So cool, in fact, that commercial lenders have always lobbied against the program. After all, they have lost a lot of business to the ODVA over the years. At one time the ODVA held mortgages on one out of every eight Oregon homes — the largest lender in the state. Not only that, the IRS loses a lot of income tax revenue from the investors who buy the bonds. Loss of income tax revenue is something which Congress takes very, very seriously.

Of course, real estate agents, homebuilders and veterans are powerful lobbying entities also. Nevertheless, political pressure finally resulted in curtailment of the program a few years ago. The result is that only veterans of the Vietnam War era are currently entitled. More recent veterans are eligible under Oregon law, but federal legislation must be enacted before the Oregon statute can take effect. To date that has not happened, although the ODVA keeps trying to get it through Congress.

Just in case you're entitled, the ODVA uses commercial lenders throughout the state as their agents to originate the loan. You can also apply directly through their office in Salem. Loans are either FHA insured or conventional insured loans. The loans are fixed rate loans, and the rate is usually about 1% below market. One warning — the property must remain owner-occupied. If you move out, the interest rate goes to a rate much higher than market — usually two or three percent above market.

State bond programs

Both Washington and Oregon (along with most other states) have state bond programs for first-time homebuyers. The basis of these programs is that interest income on bonds issued by a state government can be exempt from federal income tax if used for certain purposes. This makes the bonds attractive to investors, especially the big guys in the high tax brackets. They are so attractive that the investors are willing to settle for much lower interest rates than they would accept from a bank deposit or other taxable investment. The result is that the state has available a pool of funds at lower than market cost, which it can use to make loans at interest rates similarly below market. Sound good so far? If you're a first-time buyer, read on!

In Oregon the programs are administered through the Department of Housing and Community Services. In Washington the agency is the Washington State Housing Finance Commission. (Both are listed in the Resources section at the back of this book.) The programs are virtually identical, since each state takes full advantage of what federal law allows them to use the bond money for.

Both agencies purchase loans originated by institutional lenders throughout their states. Loans must be insured by the FHA, by private mortgage insurance (insured conventional loans), or guaranteed by the federal Rural Economic Development Corporation (see below). Loans can be made only to borrowers whose incomes do not exceed the median income for the area served. The median price of the home also cannot exceed the median for the area served. Borrowers cannot have owned a home for the three years immediately preceding the purchase, although this can be waived in certain targeted areas (generally economically distressed areas of the cities). The median purchase price can also be waived in targeted areas.

The state agencies set a maximum interest rate the lenders may charge on the loan. This interest rate is well below market interest rate, but above the rate the agency is paying investors who buy the bonds. Lenders are happy to make the loans at this rate because the state agency will buy the loan from them at face value (par). The lender receives the servicing contracts on the loans and the loan origination fees. Note that the state agencies are really just acting as secondary lenders.

Since bonds are sold at varying times and in varying amounts, the state agencies adjust the interest rates on the programs from time to time. The agencies also adjust the maximum loan amounts and the maximum allowable income as the median sales prices and incomes in their service areas change. The interest rates are always below market, however, making the programs desirable for first time borrowers.

The state agencies also have the authority to issue "mortgage credit certificates." These certificates entitle the borrower to a federal income tax credit of 20% of the interest they pay on their loan each year. This is in addition to the deductibility of their mortgage interest as an itemized deduction on their federal income tax. The qualifying requirements are the same as for the loan purchase programs. I want to emphasize something to make it clear here — the 20% is a tax *credit*, not a deduction from income. That is, you subtract it directly from the tax bill. If you normally get a tax refund, your refund will be larger by 20% of your mortgage interest.

Borrowers who obtain a loan through the bond sale programs cannot also obtain a mortgage credit certificate. Usually the loan program is what serves the borrower the best. However, the state agencies frequently run out of funds which force them to halt new loans until the next bond sale. In the meantime, the mortgage credit certificate program is all that is available.

Since the loans are made through institutional lenders, details of the programs are available from local lenders and mortgage brokers in each state. Each state agency will be happy to give you a list of approved lenders in their state. If local lenders say they are out of state funds at the moment, call the state agency to see if you may at least qualify for a mortgage credit certificate.

Government loan programs for rural areas

OK, this time the city folk can skip a section. But if you're interested in a home in a rural setting, pay attention! The government offers numerous advantageous loan programs for country property — and not just farms. There are programs even for single-family homes.

Although rural properties can also be financed through the FHA, the U.S. Department of Veterans Affairs, the Oregon Department of Veterans Affairs, and state mortgage bond programs, there are some federal loan programs that are specific to rural lending. In some cases these loan programs can be better for the borrower, depending on the borrower and the property, of course.

The most active of these is the Rural Economic Community Development Corporation (RECDC), formerly known as the Farmers Home Administration. The RECDC has programs which echo the way FHA works — loans are made by private institutions and are then insured or guaranteed by the RECDC. Details as to down payment, maximum loan amount, qualifying property, etc. are different from FHA, of course. Loan programs include —
- Home and farm purchase and improvement
- Construction and rehabilitation of farm homes
- Loans for low-income farmers

These loans can be sold to the Federal Agricultural Mortgage Corporation ("Farmer Mac"), which acts as a secondary lender in the same fashion as Fannie Mae, Ginnie Mae and Freddie Mac.

Loans insured or guaranteed by the RECDC can be made only in designated rural areas, which means that the property must be a certain number of miles from an incorporated town or city with a population over a certain amount. In some cases loans to purchase a rural home can be up to 100% loan to value ratio. Since these loans are usually made by institutional lenders, they would have the details to be able to advise you whether the home you want to buy is in an area which would qualify.

Conventional loans

Although we consider the FHA the oldest loan program, in reality, conventional loans are older — by thousands of years, in fact, depending on how you look at it. Before the FHA came along (1934), the term "conventional loan" didn't exist. The term was coined to distinguish ordinary loans from the new FHA insured loans. The term has continued, being used today to mean any loan that is made by a private lender without any government involvement.

Today, conventional loans outnumber government loans by a wide margin. In the past the numbers were closer to 50-50, mostly because government loans had more favorable down payment terms. Conventional loans have caught up with government loans in this respect, and offer somewhat faster closing and service, and usually considerably less paperwork. (Regardless of what loan program you end up with, you'll be astonished at the paperwork, though.)

Originally conventional loans were all fixed rate mortgages (FRMS), and these still remain the most popular today. There is something comforting in knowing that at least the principal and interest portion of you payment will not change. You can get a fixed rate mortgage today with a term of 10, 15, 20 or 30 years. The tradeoff is the size of the monthly payment vs. the shorter payoff. It's nice to think of having the house paid off in ten years, but few can afford the high monthly payments necessary to do so. After all, for a $100,000 loan at 8% for 30 years, you will pay a total of $164,155 in interest. You won't get to the halfway point in the principal balance until about 22½ years into the loan. Pretty depressing, isn't it? Makes you want to start life all over again, and this time pick parents who are really rich.

A variation on the theme is to get a bi-weekly mortgage. This means that you make a payment every other week. Although originally designed for borrowers who get paid bi-weekly, lenders and borrowers quickly discovered another advantage. By splitting the usual monthly payment in two, but making one every other week, you're really making the equivalent of 13 monthly payments a year (52 weeks in a year means there are 26 bi-weekly payments, each equal to one-half the usual monthly payment). That extra monthly payment every year has a dramatic effect on the amortization — shaving years off the final payoff date.

Of course, you could do this anyway with a regular 30-year loan. Just make an extra payment once a year. This is an ideal strategy if you receive a large Christmas bonus every year. Other borrowers dedicate their income tax refund to it. However you do it, one extra payment a year will cut as many as ten years off a 30-year loan, depending on the interest rate.

Look at the following charts to see how the different term options affect the payoff and total amount of interest over the life of the loan —

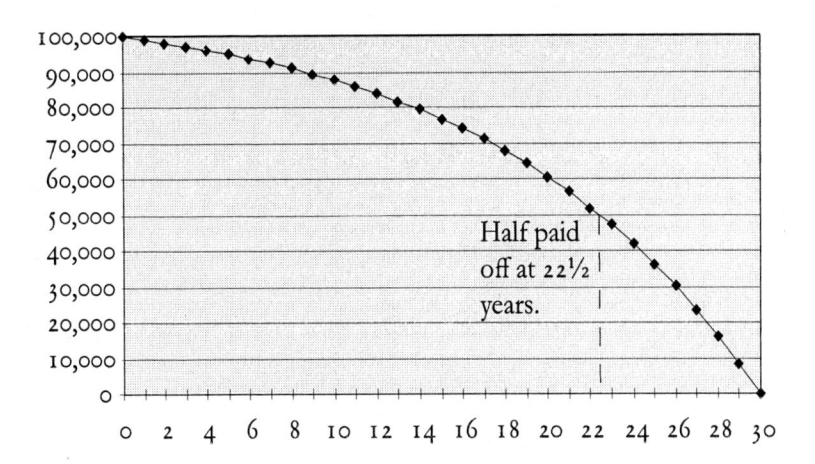

Graphic charts for 30-year regular (above), and bi-weekly (below). Notice that the bi-weekly mortgage is paid off in full at approximately 23 years, even though the borrowers make effectively the equivalent of only one additional payment each year.

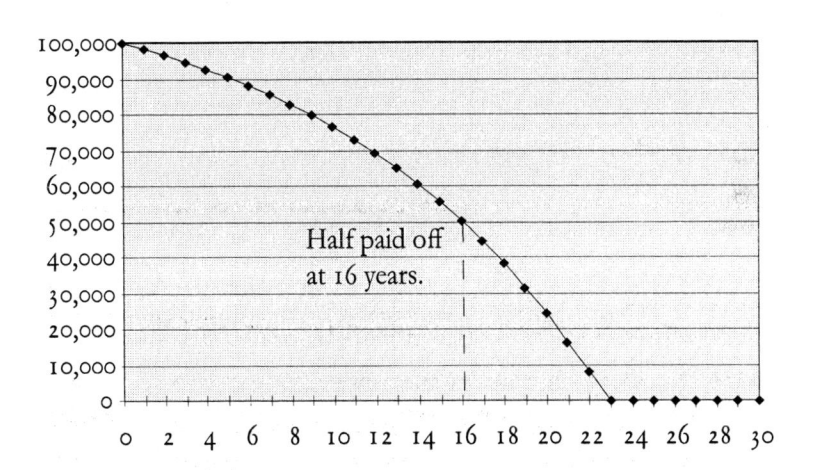

Fixed rate mortgages sometimes have balloons. A balloon is a required payoff at some point in the future, usually five or seven years. At that point you are expected to refinance. Because the lender knows it won't be stuck for more than a few years in the event of rising interest rates, you can usually get a much more attractive interest rate than for a regular FRM.

Another variation is an FRM with a balloon, plus a rollover clause. The rollover clause allows the borrower the option to renew the loan at the point of the balloon. The renewal rate will be tied to some index plus a margin. The lender typically requires that the loan be current, that the index plus margin does not exceed some predetermined amount, and that the property be still owner-occupied.

Some borrowers who have lots of money for a down payment prefer a "no-doc" or "stated income" FRM. The idea is that you make a down payment so large that the lender doesn't feel the need to bother checking your credit, income and anything other than the appraisal of the property. Usually the absolute minimum to qualify is 20% down, and some lenders require as much as 30% down. Such loans are ideal for self-employed borrowers who usually have difficulty demonstrating their income.

Adjustable rate mortgages (ARMs) are a lower-cost alternative to FRMs. Everyone knows that interest rates in the marketplace fluctuate. Lenders have to pay interest to their investors, and the higher the interest rate in the marketplace, the higher the lender's cost of funds. By tying your mortgage interest to an index, the lender is protected against red ink. To gain this protection, the lender offers much lower interest rates on ARMs than on FRMs. Of course, this is a gamble. By getting an ARM, you are gambling that rates will not go up. If you get an FRM, you are gambling that they will.

Of course, there are other considerations. With an ARM, the payments are lower, so you can afford a more expensive house. This means you can make a bigger investment, which makes your profits larger when you resell. For example, at an average annual increase in value of 8% (typical for the northwest over the past 20 years), a $100,000 house increases in value $8,000 a year and a $150,000 house increases in value by $12,000 a year. The higher the price of the house, the bigger the dollar amount of profit, all other things being equal. Even if that is not a consideration, there are some buyers whose incomes are low enough that they need an ARM in order to be able to afford any house at all.

In spite of the potential interest savings on ARMs, FRMs remain more popular. Even in times of high interest rates, people tend to prefer the FRM. Lenders push ARMs because they don't like to gamble either. To help market the ARM, they include various features to make them less scary.

For example, all ARM loans today have some kind of interest rate cap. Usually there are both *annual caps* and *lifetime caps*, meaning that the rate cannot increase more than a certain percent in any one year (typically 2%) and no more than some other percent over the life of the loan (usually 5-6%). Some ARMs also have payment caps — in case the interest rate increase causes the payment to increase too much in any one year, the payment will be kept artificially low and the unpaid interest will accrue as negative amortization temporarily. Usually a payment cap is set at a maximum of 7½% increase from one year to the next — that is, next year's payment cannot be more than 107.5% of this year's payment.

Another sales gimmick is to offer a *teaser rate*. A teaser rate is a special introductory rate well below market, usually just for the first year. Borrowers who don't take the time to do the math go for these, thinking they are getting a good deal. What usually happens is the lender makes up for the first year loss by charging somewhat higher rates for the remaining years, usually sufficiently higher so the borrower ends up paying more overall than if there had been no teaser rate in the first place. However, in some cases teaser rates can help you get approved if the lender will qualify based on the lower payments for the first year.

The *adjustment period* varies also. Some lenders write their ARMs so they can adjust the interest as often as every month. Others settle for adjusting it only once a year, or even longer. A six-month or one-year adjustment period is typical today, but you can find all kinds of adjustment periods.

You also find ARMs tied to different indexes. Probably the most popular today is the Cost of Funds Index (COFI), which is the average cost of funds in the 11th District of the Federal Reserve Bank. Another popular index is the LIBOR rate (London Interbank Offered Rate, similar to the U.S. Federal Reserve discount rate). You also occasionally find loans tied to various U.S. treasury bill rates. The index used doesn't really matter much. Capital is now a worldwide commodity, and interest rates on one investment move pretty much the same as for other investments.

Regardless of the index on the loan, there will be a *margin*. The margin is a constant rate, usually one or two percent, to be added to the index. Think of it as the lender's cushion. Suppose you agree to an ARM tied to the COFI, which at the time is at 5%. Suppose also that your margin is 2%. Then your current interest rate will be 7%. Now, if the COFI goes up to 5½%, your interest rate will go to 7½%. The margin remains the same —

$$\frac{\begin{array}{r}Index \\ + Margin\end{array}}{= Interest\ rate}$$

If you agree to a slightly higher interest rate, you can get an ARM with a conversion privilege. This allows you to convert the loan to an FRM at some point in the future. When interest rates were high but declining, these were very popular because borrowers thought they would get the best of both worlds. When they read the fine print they discovered several problems. First, many could exercise their conversion privilege only within 30 days or so of an interest rate adjustment point, and the privilege expired altogether after the loan was a couple years old. And even if they managed to hit the window correctly, they discovered that when they converted they did not convert to an FRM at their current rate, but rather at their lender's current rate for new FRM loans — always a percent or two higher than what they were paying at the time they elected to convert.

There are also loans which are sort of the reverse of the conversion privilege, that is, fixed rate loans which convert automatically to an adjustable at some point in the future, usually one, three, five, seven or ten years into the loan.

A few lenders offer ARM loans which are interest only for a period of time, sometimes as long as the first ten years of the loan. Although few borrowers would be interested, if you have something else to invest your money in that would pay a rate more attractive than the interest you would be saving by amortizing the loan, such a loan could be advantageous.

Chapter 5, Have I Got a Program for You!

There are also lenders who will let you take an investment portfolio and pledge it as collateral for a loan to be used as the down payment. Thus you can continue to watch a stock portfolio go up with the market instead of having to liquidate it for the down payment to buy a house. Usually you can borrow only about half the value of the portfolio due to federal margin requirements.

Conventional lenders insist on insurance on all loans over 80% loan to value ratio, which is what most first-time buyers will end up with. Some lenders even insure loans over 75% loan to value ratio. The insurance is written by private mortgage insurance companies. The borrower is expected to pay the premiums for this insurance. Some lenders may say they do not charge for mortgage insurance, but check their rates carefully. Lenders have a habit of saying they do not charge for something, and then raise the interest or some other fee to compensate when your back is turned.

There are eight private mortgage insurance companies in the United States. Each has slightly different approval requirements and premiums. Some will also allow you to drop the insurance after a certain number of years or after the house goes up in value to a certain point. They are listed in the Resources section at the back of this book so you can contact them yourself.

Whether the loan is fixed rate or adjustable, sometimes it is advantageous for the borrower to get a "combination" loan. These are loans where the seller carries a second mortgage for part of the purchase price. Typical would be an 80% first mortgage, the seller carries a second mortgage for an additional 10%, and the buyer makes a down payment for the last 10% (called an 80-10-10 loan).

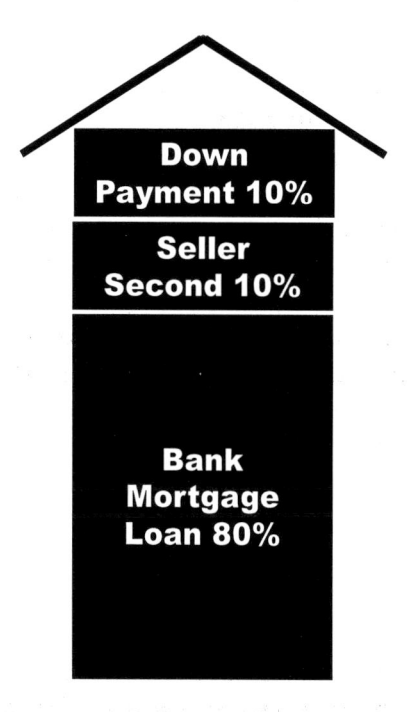

```
        Down
    Payment 10%
       Seller
    Second 10%


        Bank
      Mortgage
      Loan 80%
```

The advantage is that, by getting a loan with a low loan to value ratio, the borrower's costs on the first are much lower — low enough to compensate for having to pay somewhat higher interest to the seller on the second. The cost savings will come from slightly lower interest rate and savings on the private mortgage insurance (most lenders do not require private mortgage insurance on loans at 80% loan to value ratio and under). Private mortgage insurance can cost thousands, so eliminating it is a major financial gain. Not only that, the loan can be closed more quickly and easily. The second will usually be short term anyway, so the total cost to the borrower can be lower than for a straight 90% first.

Assuming a loan

Taking over the sellers' old loan is a time-honored way of buying. In most areas of the northwest we call this an assumption, but some places people call it "cash to the loan."

There are definite advantages to assuming the seller's old loan. The major benefit is cost savings. A new conventional loan today will typically cost a 2% loan origination fee, and FHA and VA loan origination fees are 1%. When you assume you will be expected to pay an assumption fee, but the amount is generally half what a new loan origination fee would be. Right there you save in the neighborhood of $1,000. But that is not all. When you assume you will not have to pay for an appraisal or a lender's title insurance policy — add another $500 or so in savings.

Taking over the sellers' old loan is somewhat more difficult than it used to be because most loans made in the past ten to fifteen years include a due on sale clause. Of course, another problem is that the seller typically has more equity than you can afford to pay for in cash. If you're buying a house for $125,000, chances are the seller's loan balance is less than $100,000. That means you need to come up with $25,000 or more in cash to buy the house. Finding a house with an assumable loan where the seller's equity is small enough to be affordable is not easy.

Still, you do run into it once in a while. It's also possible for the seller to carry a second to help you out. And it's also possible for you to obtain a second on your own from another lender. An excellent source of second mortgage loans for such purposes is a credit union. Credit unions are usually smaller lenders and find it difficult to get into the first mortgage business. But they do quite a business in small second mortgage loans for their members, and at very attractive interest rates and terms.

The first step in assuming a loan is for the sellers to determine if their old loan is assumable or not. If it is an FHA or federal GI loan, I can assure you that it is, and that the lender is prohibited from raising the interest rate on assumption. If it is a conventional loan the sellers or their agent will have to call the lender. For conventional loans usually the terms of the loan allow the lender to increase the interest rate to market. This frequently makes it undesirable for the buyer to assume it, but there are occasional exceptions, particularly if it is an ARM loan.

If it is a private contract or trust deed, the only way to find out if it is assumable is to get a copy of the actual document. Since all such documents are recorded, you can easily get a copy from the county recorder's office or from the customer service department of a title insurance company, even if the sellers can't find their copy.

You may occasionally hear people use the term "blind assumption." Usually this means that you can take over the sellers' old loan without going through credit approval. Practically all assumable loans today allow the lender to demand that a buyer qualify, so blind assumptions are pretty unusual. About the only time you can get away without credit approval is if the sellers' old loan is from a private party. Even then, more often than not, the document has a clause prohibiting assumption without the private party's approval.

Seller financing

If the seller is willing to carry the paper, you can make any deal you can get the seller to agree to. All the techniques used by conventional lenders can be used here too. For example, if the payment is too high, you can make the interest rate adjustable to get the seller to agree to lower it. Anything goes.

Although you can make any deal you want, beware of violating the KISS principle — KISS stands for "Keep It Simple, Stupid." The problem is getting the seller's acceptance. The more convoluted your offer, the more afraid of it the seller will become. Use whatever things you need in order to make the terms work for you, but don't use any more than you have to. The simpler, the better.

One really nice thing about seller financing is that it is fast. Once you make the offer and the seller accepts, you're ready to go to closing. No waiting around for a lender to approve the loan and prepare the documents.

When making your offer you should consider a bit of psychology. Sellers are very sensitive to price. They are also sensitive to the interest rate you are offering, but less so. Therefore, as a rule, to make a good deal, lower the interest rate before you lower the price. As far as your pocketbook is concerned, it need not make any difference if you calculate the terms right.

For example, suppose you have $10,000 for the down payment and you are considering buying a house listed for $110,000. Assume market interest rates at the time are about 9%. If you buy it for $100,000 (cutting the price by $10,000), owing the seller $90,000 at 9% interest for 30 years, you will make 360 payments of $724.16, or a total of $260,697 over the life of the contract. Adding the down payment of $10,000, your total cost for the house is $270,697.

Now take the same property with the same down payment and offer the seller the full listed price of $110,000, a loan balance of $100,000 instead of $90,000, and an interest rate of 8.4% instead of 9%. With a 30-year period, your payments come out to $723.74 — practically the same. Over the 30 years this comes to $260,548 in payments. Adding the down payment of $10,000 means your total cost for the house is $270,548 — virtually the same amount. Yet you were able to offer the seller the listed price for the house instead of cutting it by $10,000.

Which do you think the seller would be more sensitive to, cutting the price by $10,000, or offering an interest rate six tenths of a percent lower than market? When making offers with seller financing, always remember that the price and the interest rate are related to each other. You can compensate for one by adjusting the other.

If you've read through this entire chapter, you're probably confused. There are so many programs, it's just about impossible to know which is the best for you. Don't worry. A good lender knows these programs up one side and down the other. And if you go to a mortgage broker, practically all of them are able to make any of these loans, they will know which is most likely to work best for you.

All you need to do is watch out for sharks. To be sure you end up with a reputable lender, read the chapter on predatory lenders. Once you have a lender you can trust, the task of financing will get lots less confusing. Eventually you'll know the joy of sending off a mortgage payment every month just like the rest of us!

Credit is a system whereby a person who can't pay gets another person who can't pay to guarantee that he can pay.
CHARLES DICKENS

Chapter 6

Honest, I Can Handle the Payments!

Convincing the lender to grant you the loan is the most nerve-wracking part of buying a house. It's a lot better these days than it used to be, though. At least nowadays you are usually working with a mortgage broker who is being paid on a commission basis. This means the person you are dealing with doesn't get paid unless you get the loan — a lot better than the old days when the lender played God with you directly.

Still, at some point there is an omnipotent entity who must approve your loan. Whether it is the "loan committee" a "senior loan officer," or "head office" — somewhere there is a supreme being who must pass judgment on your humble application for thirty years of servitude. In a way this is even worse. In the old days you could at least go down to the bank and pound your shoe on the loan officer's desk. Now everything is removed. People making the final credit decisions no longer have to dirty their hands dealing directly with common borrowers.

The first step in this process is to become preapproved. You should do this even before you start looking at houses. After all, what seller will accept your offer to buy without some assurance that you are qualified?

These days we make a distinction between being "prequalified" and being "preapproved." Being prequalified means a letter from a mortgage broker that, based on the income you represented, you should be qualified for a loan of a certain amount of money to buy a house. The letter says it is only an opinion, and subject to credit report, income verification and appraisal of the property. In other words, the lender did little more than sign a form letter, filling in an amount obtained by doing a couple quick calculations based on your own statements.

If that is what you get from a lender, move on. You need "preapproval," which is much more involved. When a lender preapproves you they will at least run part of the approval process, like the credit report. They may charge you for the credit report, but you will have a preapproval letter that will be respected by real estate agents in the area. Most will also go through income verification and other things that must be determined. The result is a letter saying they will lend you a certain amount of money with the sole contingency of the appraisal. Agents generally know which lenders take preapproval letters seriously and which ones do a shoddy job of it.

I should caution you that this is an area where you should be careful. There are lenders out there who issue preapproval letters that are mostly blue sky. They're hoping you will choose them because they think you're good for a bigger loan than their competitors do. Of course, if you buy a house and then apply for a loan in the amount of their "opinion," all of a sudden their tune changes. Knowing they cannot get you the loan they promised you, they make excuse after excuse, hoping that eventually you'll borrow money from mom and dad to get a bigger down payment, agree to a higher interest rate, or do something else to put the deal together. They know the typical buyer doesn't want to lose his or her dream house. In the end, they get the loan. They make their commission. Everyone else is furious, but they got theirs and that's all they care about. The bottom line is: Choose your preapproval lender with care and a bit of skepticism.

Once you have a final contract with a seller for the house you're going to buy, it's time for the real loan application. The application process will take a couple of hours, so make sure your appointment is for sometime when you won't have to rush off in the middle. The loan officer you will be dealing with will give you a list of things to get together before your appointment. This will be things like pay stubs and other data regarding income, plus information about your current loans and other monthly expenses. You will also be expected to bring a check for the credit report, which usually costs about $25 to $50.

Credit reports

Now we need to take a moment and discuss your credit report. There are various kinds of credit reports, and there are different credit reporting agencies. Your lender will be ordering a "full mortgage credit report," which goes into considerably more detail than just a computer printout of what the credit bureau has on you. For example, they check court records to see if anyone has sued you to collect money. They want to know everything.

Lots of borrowers worry about derogatory information in their credit report. My advice is to get a copy of your credit report yourself and review it. You should probably do this before you start looking at houses and even before you get a preapproval letter. There are three main credit reporting agencies — Experian (formerly TRW), TransUnion, and Equifax. Each will mail you a copy of your credit report for a fee of about $8. Since each maintains a separate file, you should check all three for errors. Their addresses and web sites are listed in the Resources section at the back of this book.

If you find errors in the credit report you have various options. The ideal solution is just to have the creditor who supplied the erroneous information correct it. Surprisingly, sometimes this works. Sometimes it takes a long time, though. And some creditors are less than courteous about it. Once I had to have a borrower get his attorney to write the creditor a letter before we got action. Since the borrower was about to lose an important deal if the incorrect information was not fixed, the attorney was able to threaten punitive damages. The creditor ignored my client until the letter from the attorney, but that finally got their attention. Note that the credit bureau itself is untouchable — they are just reporting what the creditor says and have no liability. It's the creditor you have to get hold of around the neck.

Sometimes there is something that you just can't do anything about. Like, what if the derogatory information is true? Naturally, you won't be able to get the information out of your file, but you still have one card left to play. The Fair Credit Reporting Act allows you to send the credit bureau a letter explaining the facts and they must place the letter in your file, and include a copy of it with each report they send out. For some reason, borrowers are frequently reluctant to take this step. Nevertheless, it makes no sense to leave the issue unexplained. At least if there is a letter in your file you can state your side of the issue. It's also a signal to future creditors that you take your credit seriously.

There is another dimension to bad credit. I have had borrowers approved for loans even when they had what appeared to be horrible credit. Once, many years ago, I was approached by a man who wanted to buy a house. He needed a large house, as he was single but had seven kids. He was also really short on down payment. I figured I could get him into a house with FHA financing, although it might be a tight squeeze. I agreed to work with him, mostly because he was really eager to buy a house. I could tell that his real motivation was the kids — he wanted them to have a home of their own.

We looked at houses for a week or so, and then finally we settled on one that suited his needs — a huge older house with eight bedrooms. He made an offer and I got the seller to accept it. The next day he made an appointment for the loan application with a loan officer I recommended.

A few days later I got a call from the loan officer. It seems his credit report had just come in, and it was terrible. Every single account showed several months of past due payments. To top it all, he had filed bankruptcy six months earlier, and it had been final just a month before he came to see me.

I was shocked. People with such horrible credit don't go out and waste their own and everyone else's time trying to buy a house. Or if they do, at least they level with the real estate agent and look for seller contracts or something where they have half a chance of getting the property.

I called the buyer and gave him the bad news. He sounded really dejected, but just sighed and said "I guess I can't buy a house then." He thanked me for my efforts and said goodbye.

It still didn't set right with me. Something was wrong. It didn't add up. After a few hours stewing about it (and I still hadn't called the seller with the news), I called the buyer back. I pried a little, but he wouldn't give me anything further. Finally I convinced him to make an appointment and go see the loan officer again. I knew the loan officer, and I knew she was as professional as they come. If anyone could do anything, she could.

His appointment was for the next day early in the afternoon. About 4:00 the loan officer called me. She said it took her nearly an hour, but she finally found out what was going on. It seems his wife had spent the previous four years dying of cancer. The medical expenses had not only wiped them out, but he had also been unable to pay other bills on time because he was paying the doctors to keep her alive. When she finally died he owed so much money he had no choice but to file bankruptcy. By the time the loan officer got the story out of him he was in tears.

She took a piece of paper and set it in front of him. She said, "you just write that down and sign it. I'll get you that house if it's the last thing I do."

One month and three days later the buyer and his seven kids moved into their new house, complete with FHA mortgage. On moving day I had to go by and say hi. All the kids could talk about was being able to have their own bedrooms. The look on their faces was worth ten times as much as the commission check.

Don't ever assume that only people with squeaky-clean credit reports can buy a house.

Credit repair

These days credit repair agencies plaster their advertising everywhere. To read their hype you'd think they could take a guy in receivership and give him a credit report that look like he's Bill Gates. While it is possible to fix errors in a credit report (see above), the things some of these outfits promise to do are mostly either illegal or impossible. And what little they can do, you can do for yourself for free anyway.

For example, one tactic the credit repair scammers tell you to do is to apply to the IRS for an Employer Identification Number

(EIN), then use this number when applying. Supposedly this will give you a brand new, unblemished credit report. Probably it will. But this is illegal. You may not enjoy the clean credit report much when you are discovered, because you'll be in jail.

Mostly all these outfits do is send creditors letters to see if they will remove or upgrade derogatory information. Sometimes this does work. But you could have done this yourself and saved the hundreds of dollars the credit repair agencies charge.

Credit scoring

Borrowers are terrified of credit scoring these days. For some reason everyone has the idea that it is like a college board exam — if you don't measure up to the mark on the wall you don't get to play with the big boys and girls. This is simply not true. Nowadays you can get financing, frequently even prime financing, even if you have a relatively low score. Just as colleges do not use the college board scores as the only criterion for admissions, lenders do not rely entirely on your point score.

Credit scoring started in the 1970's when lenders first had to face the Equal Credit Opportunity Act. Lenders were afraid that the new law would make them liable for lawsuits from minorities and women. A point scoring system sounded nice and safe. You make the grade or you don't. As long as the criteria for the scoring system are not based on illegal discrimination issues, lenders felt safe.

Of course, lenders are no longer afraid of the discrimination laws. But over time they learned that there are definite benefits to point scoring. It removes the a lot of the personal bias of the loan officer, for example.

For real estate loans, point scoring is done today based on a statistical analysis system originated by Fair, Isaac Company (commonly referred to as the FICO score). All three national credit bureaus do it the same way, although they call it by different names — Equifax calls it the "Beacon," Trans Union calls it "Empirica" and Experian uses the original name "Fair, Isaac." The score is reported in a range from 350 to 900 points. A score of zero means there was insufficient data in your credit file to generate a score.

Here are some samples of how the statistics work out —
- Scores below 601 yield eight good loans for each bad one.
- Scores between 700 and 729 yield 129 good loans for each bad one.
- Scores above 800 yield 1,292 good loans for each bad one.

Creditors, of course, receive the full statistical breakdown, so they can assess the exact odds that a given score will be a good loan.

Among professional lenders, however, "FICO" has come to be a dirty word. It's purpose is just to alert the lender that more investigation is in order. Unfortunately, a lot of lenders just go by the score and do little else. You measure up to the statistical level they demand, or you are denied. And that's it. There is no recourse; no appeal.

Professional lenders know that the FICO score is just statistics, nothing more. Statistics lie a lot. The Fair, Isaac Company created their models based on various criteria, but those issues don't necessarily apply in all cases. For example, although the Fair, Isaac Company maintains their statistical models as proprietary, they have disclosed that they use five categories —
- Previous credit history
- Current amount of debt
- Amount of time the borrower has used credit
- How often the borrower has made applications for credit
- Types of credit available

Let's look at those criteria for a minute. Look, for example, at how often the borrower has made applications for credit. Now, I can understand that, if a borrower is applying all over town, it is a possible indication that the borrower is desperate, making a last-ditch attempt to borrow money to stave off default or bankruptcy. But it also might mean nothing at all. The statistical model can't know *why* the borrower was making credit applications. All it knows is how many, and it makes an assumption based on that figure alone. Unfortunately, the credit bureau will furnish your mortgage lender just the final FICO point score, with no explanation of how the score was derived. Professionals know that the score is not necessarily a correct indicator.

How can I improve my FICO score?

Of course, even if you have a professional lender, it certainly wouldn't hurt if you have a higher FICO score. There are a few things you can do that might improve your score —

- Pay credit card accounts down to no more than 50% of the highest balance you ever had
- Close any account where you ever made a late payment
- Close all but a couple of your revolving charge accounts (e.g., Sears, Bon Marché, etc.)
- Avoid letting anyone make credit inquiries on you
- Pay off any outstanding collection accounts against you
- Write dispute letters to the credit bureau on any derogatory information that you disagree with.

It will take a while for these measures to take effect, so do it immediately.

Scoring classifications

Mortgage lenders speak of "prime" and "subprime" credit, or sometimes use terms like "an A loan," "a B loan," and so on. Mostly these terms are based on the FICO score. For example, a score of 670 or higher is considered A+, 650 to 669 is an A loan, 620 to 649 is a B loan, and so on. Anything lower than an A rating would be considered subprime.

An A+ loan would be funded at the best interest rates available. Credit approval would be completed very quickly. An A loan would also get a good interest rate, but would take a little longer to approve because the lender would need to investigate derogatory information in the credit file. Loans with a B rating cannot be sold to Fannie Mae or Freddie Mac, so the lender will have to find an alternative secondary lender. This will make the interest rate higher. And verification of credit will take even longer as well.

Qualifying ratios

Lenders use two income qualifying ratios. First, they take your total housing costs and divide it by your total gross monthly income. This is called the "housing cost ratio," or more commonly by the slang expression, the "front end ratio." For example, sup-

Chapter 6, Honest, I Can Handle the Payments! 131

pose you are applying for a loan of $100,000 at 8% for 30 years, and the annual property taxes on the house are $1,800 and the annual fire insurance premium is $480. The total housing cost breakdown will be —

Monthly principal and interest	$733.76
One-twelfth the tax bill	150.00
One-twelfth the fire insurance premium	40.00
Total	$923.76

Now suppose you have an annual gross income of $42,000, which is to say, $3,500 a month. You take the housing cost of $923.76 and divide it by the monthly income of $3,500 to get the housing cost ratio. In this example, it comes out as 26.39% ($923.75 divided by $3,500 = 0.2639).

A housing cost ratio of 26.39% would qualify you for any loan program. Most lenders allow housing cost ratios up to 28-29%

The second ratio is the "total debt service ratio," also called the "back end ratio." This is the total payments you are making, including the proposed mortgage payment. "Total payments" means payments on debt, not utility bills, car insurance, etc. Using the above example, suppose you had a monthly car payment of $150 and credit card payments of $100. The breakdown would be —

Monthly principal and interest	$733.76
One-twelfth the tax bill	150.00
One-twelfth the fire insurance premium	40.00
Car payment	150.00
Credit card payments	100.00
Total debt service	$1,173.76

Dividing the total debt service by the monthly gross income gives us a total debt service ratio of 33.53% ($1,173.76 divided by $3,500 = 0.3353). Most lenders will allow a total debt service ratio of 36%, and some will go as high as 41%.

These two ratios are not hard and fast lines drawn in the sand. If you score a little too high on one, but lower on the other, the loan will still probably be approved. It just depends on the overall picture. If you are above both limits you may be still approved if your FICO score is high, your employment history is unusually stable, and/or you have good prospects for increased income.

Income, what qualifies and what does not

Income is one of the more troublesome areas of loan underwriting. For some borrowers (e.g., self-employed) it can be extremely difficult due to problems with verification. But even for people with more normal employment there are various considerations.

Lenders take a look at your income from two perspectives — quantity and reliability. If a source of income is unreliable, it should be disregarded. For example, should we include income from overtime pay? Most lenders do, but some lenders do only if the borrower demonstrates a pattern of always receiving a certain amount. Usually the lender will take the average over the past couple of years, and only with verification from the employer that it is likely to continue.

Alimony and child support can usually be counted as income. Most lenders require evidence that it will continue for at least three years after the loan is made, usually by providing the lender with a copy of the divorce decree or settlement. As with all income, it must be verified by deposit slips or bank statements.

Other kinds of income are treated on an individual basis. Anything that cannot be demonstrated by a third party (e.g., an employer), will have to be verified by tax returns or some other means. Regardless of the income, you generally have to demonstrate that you have received it for the preceding two years.

The collateral — getting the property appraised

In the past the appraisal process has been anywhere from a piece of cake to a nightmare. The problem is that the federal government decided to get involved in it. You can imagine what happened after that. Today appraisers are highly regulated. Most of the regulations accomplish nothing more than increase the cost of an appraisal.

Twenty years ago the only problems we had with appraisals were that they were sometimes a little slow and sometimes the appraiser didn't think the property was worth what the buyer was paying. Today things are more complicated.

The appraiser is the agent of the lender, not the borrower. You are expected to pay the fee, but the appraiser is working for the bank, not you. Therefore, appraisers felt (and they were legally correct in doing so) that the borrower was not entitled to a copy of the appraisal report. This allowed the bank to play games with the appraisal report. For example, if the lender didn't want to make the loan, rather than just honestly turn you down, the lender would say "it didn't appraise for enough." And all the time there was an appraisal report in the lender's file saying the property was worth plenty to support the loan.

Things have changed. Due to serious screaming by borrowers and real estate agents, Congress enacted legislation requiring the lender to supply you with a copy of the appraisal report if you are the one who paid for it. Now you can tell what the appraiser really said. No more games blaming the appraiser when the bank wants to turn down the loan.

If you have ever seen an appraisal report, you will realize why they take several days to complete. A typical report today will run to six or seven double-sided legal size forms, with hundreds of bits of information the appraiser has to fill out. There must be a photograph of the house as well as other exhibits. Getting all this stuff together takes some time. Most appraisers batch their work — that is, they do four or five appraisals at a time. One day they go out and inspect all the properties. The next day they get the verifications and other data together. And then they spend a day writing up all the reports. It's not like they get the order for your appraisal and immediately drop everything and go out and do it from start to finish for you. That would be a very inefficient way to work.

Many lenders today can accept a "limited assignment" appraisal that is less expensive than a full assignment appraisal. Mostly it means the appraiser skips the interior inspection. The going rate for a full assignment appraisal is about $400 to $450; the limited assignment is about $100 cheaper. It's something to ask about when you apply for the loan.

If there's anything I hope I got across to you in this chapter it's that you need a *professional* loan officer, not a paper-shuffling robot. Anyone can go by the book. It takes someone experienced, knowledgeable and dedicated to look behind the issues and find out what's really important. Don't settle for a lender who just goes by the numbers. Interview several lenders and find one who understands the mortgage business and how to make credit decisions.

Avoid taking recommendations from others. Even a recommendation from your real estate agent is suspect. Frankly, real estate agents — even buyers' agents — are not very knowledgeable about the mortgage business. "I've had good service from ABC Mortgage Company" means the transactions closed, which is all the agent cares about. Whether the borrower got the best loan possible or is satisfied with the service is not something the agent knows or has any interest in. The only way to find a good lender is shop for yourself.

Banks will lend you money if you can prove you don't need it.
MARK TWAIN

Chapter 7

Beware the Predatory Lender!

What is a predatory lender? Most borrowers are shocked to discover that a mortgage lender may be less than honest. We are so accustomed to hearing about borrowers defaulting on their obligations to lenders, that it never occurs to us that lenders might not be 100% forthright with borrowers.

Yet that is exactly what is happening today. Things are so bad that the industry has even coined the term "predatory lenders" to describe lenders who take advantage of borrowers. Although first-time buyers are not the primary target of predatory lenders, there are abuses all borrowers need to be aware of.

Defining what is a predatory lender is a bit difficult. No one in the industry has an official definition. Most think it is only when a lender does something especially bad. Minor sins don't seem to upset people. To me, any practice that tries to pull the wool over the borrower's eyes for the lender's profit should be considered predatory. But then, I have never lost a lot of love on lenders.

The worst problems so far have been with refinance loans, chiefly targeted at cash-poor minorities and senior citizens who have a high equity in their homes. The usual practice is to lend them money using high pressure sales tactics, at high interest rates and high loan fees, preying on their need for cash.

This isn't bad enough, however. After the loan has been on the books for a few months the lender calls the borrower back and says they can now qualify for a much better loan. Of course there will be new loan fees for the refinance. There are reports of borrowers who have been churned five or six times, all their equity in the property has been eaten up in loan fees, and they are facing foreclosure. Getting the borrower to refinance over and over is called "loan flipping," a practice that is decried by reputable lenders.

One of the techniques used to promote loan flipping is to write loans with balloon payments. This ensures that the borrower has no choice but to refinance. Of course, the original lender is there waiting, helpfully offering an easy solution to the borrower pressured to meet the balloon. Naturally, the "easy solution" will further line the lender's pockets with additional fees and charges.

The borrowers most vulnerable to predatory lenders are those with subprime credit. Unable to obtain financing elsewhere, they jump at the chance to borrow. Predatory lenders solicit these borrowers by deliberately targeting advertising toward them. Some predatory lenders have even been known to send salespeople door to door, targeting certain neighborhoods looking for borrowers.

Part of the problem is that there is no easy way to determine what is predatory lending and what is merely subprime lending. Every year $150 to $200 billion in subprime mortgages are created. For most borrowers, this is a valuable service. Halting subprime lending altogether would disenfranchise marginal borrowers and block their ability to improve their lives. Everyone condemns predatory lending, and in the same breath encourages subprime lending as being of great benefit to low-income borrowers and people getting back on their feet after being financially distressed.

When you use the term "predatory lender" many in the lending industry think the foregoing is all it refers to. As a first-time buyer you are not the biggest target of predatory lenders because you have not yet built up a big equity in a home. Nevertheless, predatory lenders go after you as well. They know you have never applied for a mortgage loan before and have no idea how the industry works. Using their knowledge of lending practices makes it easy for them to take advantage of you.

With first-time borrowers the usual tactic is to convince you that you cannot qualify for a prime loan, and therefore you need to pay a higher interest rate, higher loan fee, bigger discount, agree to a prepayment penalty, or something else which will line the lender's pockets more luxuriously.

A scam is successful only if the mark believes the con artist. When the lender says your credit is less than perfect, you are especially vulnerable. We are our own worst critics — everyone believes his or her credit is worse than it really is. You remember the times when you paid a bill late. It's easy to assume the worst. The reality is that, most of the time, minor problems like that weren't even reported by the creditor. A lot of people are surprised to discover they have perfect credit reports. It's easy for a predatory lender to get a first-time buyer to believe that his or her credit is substandard.

Another common tactic used with first-time mortgage borrowers is to delay closing until a rate lock expires. There are simple things the lender can do to accomplish this. For example, the lender can simply call for a review of the appraisal, guaranteed to add at least a week to the processing time. Or the lender can call you up and say that the underwriter needs some additional documentation from you. I have had lenders just not send the documents out. When I called to ask why the documents weren't at the escrow ready for the borrower's signature, I was told they had already been sent. Of course, they hadn't been sent. They hadn't even been typed yet. But the loan officer lied in order to buy some time.

After a few days of trying to find the "missing" documents, they agreed to "retype" them. But when the documents arrived at the escrow, the interest rate was 3/8 of a percent higher than the rate the borrower had locked in. When we complained, the lender said "too bad, your rate lock expired and I have no choice." The borrower was sitting there, the notice on his apartment was up, the seller had moved out, and he had no alternative but to go ahead and sign.

There is an even greater evil lurking for borrowers with rate locks. Occasionally a borrower will pay for a rate lock, but the loan officer will not lock the rate, hoping that rates will come down before closing and the loan officer can pocket a premium. Although fraudulent, it will work if the loan officer calls the market correctly and rates do come down. But what if rates go up instead? The loan officer should eat the loss, but some can't afford to do it.

The loan officer simply defaults on the rate lock and tells the borrower "I have no choice." The borrower is back sitting at the escrow with a higher interest rate and no real recourse. Sure you can sue the loan officer, but why should you have to go through that? And besides, even if you do, if the loan officer doesn't have the money to eat the loss, chances are there won't be any funds to collect your judgment from, either.

Predatory lenders don't care who they take advantage of. Once I was selling a property where the buyers were getting a new loan. The paperwork was all ready at the escrow, except my lender insisted that the loan had a prepayment penalty and was demanding nearly $2,800 additional for the payoff. I knew that the loan didn't have a prepayment penalty and complained to the lender. I even got copies of the recorded documents myself and went over them line by line. There was no prepayment penalty. Nevertheless, the lender as much as said "too bad, we're not going to release your old mortgage unless you pay it, whether the prepayment penalty is in the agreement or not." They were assuming that I needed the cash from the sale and would eat the $2,800 to get the deal closed. Instead I discussed it with the title insurance company. Based on the fact that my loan documents did not contain a prepayment penalty, they agreed to close without paying my lender the extra $2,800. How many sellers, though, would have the knowledge and courage to do this? Most would probably just knuckle under and pay it.

Here are some warning signals to alert you that you may be dealing with a predatory lender —

- Advertising that targets poor credit risks, the elderly, or people likely to have a high equity in a home.
- Offering to present your loan application with credit and income data that stretches the truth.
- Suggesting that it is acceptable to borrow more than the property is worth.
- Requiring credit life and/or disability insurance (there's nothing wrong with it as long as it's optional).
- Fees that are higher than other lenders in the area charge for the same kind of loan.

Chapter 7, Beware the Predatory Lender!   139

- Suggesting that your credit is substandard.
- Anything that suggests the lender is delaying closing to get past a rate lock.
- A loan officer not willing to put a rate lock in writing.

Reputable lenders have called for legislation to halt predatory lending practices. Suggestions include placing restrictions on exorbitant up-front loan fees, banning prepayment penalties, not allowing credit life and disability insurance to be issued by the lender (or a subsidiary of the lender) and paid in full up front, limit-

ing interest rates (federal usury statutes), restricting discounts, and requiring mandatory borrower counseling. Unfortunately, to date, little has been done. Your best defense is still to be an informed borrower.

I might add a note about usury laws. In case you haven't heard about usury, it means charging more interest than the law allows. There are currently no federal usury laws at all. Oregon did away with its usury laws a number of years ago. And Washington, while it still has usury laws, sets the maximum so high that they might as well have done away with them.

You do have some assistance in the form of other federal laws that have been around a long time. The Truth in Lending Act and Federal Reserve Regulation z require lenders to disclose all the financial details of the loan, including the Annual Percentage Rate (APR) and the Total Finance Charge. Don't sign a loan application unless you have read and understood these disclosures thoroughly. You can no longer assume the final terms are what the lender represented to you verbally at the outset.

The APR must be calculated by all lenders using the same rules. This assures that it is a true gauge by which a consumer can compare one loan proposal with another. Calculating the APR is complicated, but the basic idea is that the lender must include all charges and fees that the lender requires you to pay, as though they were interest (which is then called the Total Finance Charge) — and then recalculate the interest rate based on this figure. Thus, if two lenders each charge 8% interest on the loan, but one charges a higher loan fee, the one with the higher loan fee will have to disclose a higher APR. The APR becomes a sort of "truth detector" for the consumer. Used together with the Total Finance Charge, you can tell which loan is a better deal.

Besides the Truth in Lending Act and Federal Reserve Regulation z, the Real Estate Settlement Procedures Act (RESPA) requires disclosure of anticipated closing costs, such as escrow frees, title insurance premiums, prepaid property taxes and fire insurance premiums, prorates for taxes between the buyer and the seller, and so on. The lender is not required to be accurate to the penny on these items because it is impossible to be sure about some of them until you know the exact closing date. Still, at the time of the loan application, the lender is required to give you a good faith estimate on a Uniform Settlement Statement designed by the Department of Housing and Urban Development. You are entitled

Chapter 7, Beware the Predatory Lender!

to a copy of the final closing statement at least one day before closing, on the same form, so you can compare the estimate to the final statement line by line. Few buyers use this benefit, but as a greedy home buyer, of course you will exercise your right to review the closing statement!

It should be added that RESPA was designed to encourage borrowers to shop for all the services they need when buying a home, not just financing. This includes brokerage services, title insurance and escrow, inspections, appraisals, etc. Take the spirit of the law to heart. Always be wary when someone suggests a particular provider of a service. It takes just a few phone calls to shop around and determine if the fee they want to charge you is reasonable.

A final note about disclosures — Oregon (but not Washington) has a state law requiring the lender to disclose when a loan contains a prepayment penalty. Unfortunately, the disclosure has to be made only in the loan document itself, not in a disclosure up front. This means you can't rest even on the day of closing. The closing officer will hate you for it, but read through the loan documents and make sure every feature is as it was originally represented. Regardless of what state you're in, reputable lenders should be willing to give you a blank copy of the loan document before closing so you can review the fine print at your leisure.

Many times I have gone to closing and discovered that one or more of the loan documents I was supposed to sign was not as the lender originally represented. If I had signed the documents as prepared, then I would have been stuck. Every single time I stood my ground and demanded that the lender revise the documents according to what we had agreed upon. The seller and the closing officer were usually annoyed, but since it was my nickel and not theirs, I didn't care. You should do the same.

Gentlemen, you are as fine a group of men as ever foreclosed a mortgage on a widow. I'm glad to be among you shylocks.
WILL ROGERS

Chapter 8

The Large Print Giveth and the Fine Print Taketh Away

Contracts make up an enormous portion of the law. Roughly one-fourth of the time lawyers spend in law school is taken up with the subject of contracts in one form or another. I am going to try to condense all of that into a short chapter, so my first advice about contracts is, don't think what I am telling you is going to make you anywhere close to an expert. More likely, I'm going to give you just enough for you to become really dangerous.

If you're not sure about something, seek professional advice. The Oregon Supreme Court made a statement once — "your signature on a contract is not a mere ornament." In other words, you signed it, you're stuck with it. Seek advice before signing.

That having been said, there are some fundamental features of contract law that can be extremely useful and profitable to know when making offers and counteroffers on real property.

Essentials

Let's start with some basics. All contracts must have certain elements to be enforceable. For example, with a few exceptions, a contract involving real property is not enforceable unless it is in writing, signed by the party on whom enforcement is sought, and states a consideration. Contracts not involving real estate can sometimes be enforceable without being in writing, although even then, only an idiot enters into a verbal contract for something that is important. In real estate, however, you have no choice. It has to be in writing to be enforceable.

There is one other important essential — all contracts involving buying or selling real estate must state the description of the real estate with certainty, at least by reference. This generally means the "legal description," which can take various formats depending on the property. One thing is sure, however — the street address is not adequate unless it is tied somewhere to the legal description of the property. For example, the contract might say "Lot 12, Block 13, Jones Addition to the City of Seattle, King County, Washington, commonly known as 1234 Seller Street South, Seattle, Washington." The first section is the legal description, and the last section ties the address to it. Now the rest of the contract, including any addendums and exhibits, can just use the street address.

Offers

Now that we have some of the essential elements understood, let's get into making offers. An offer is not valid unless it is in such a form that, if the seller accepted it, a binding contract would result. Therefore, a verbal offer is no offer, because the resulting contract has to be in writing (see above). Similarly, an offer that fails to state the consideration is not an offer. It must be sufficiently complete that all the seller has to do is write "I accept" and sign it in order to form a binding contract. Of course, you want to make a complete, written offer anyway. To do less will not impress the seller, something that is important if you want your offer to be accepted.

Offers can be given for any time frame you wish. You can give the seller one hour to accept, or one year, or any other time limit that suits your purposes. (For a discussion of the advisability of short time limits, see the chapter on negotiating.) Once the time limit is reached, the offer simply expires. If the seller accepts after that time, there is no contract, because there was no longer an offer to accept.

Even within the stated time frame, there are certain things that can cause the offer to be extinguished. For example, if either party dies or becomes incompetent, if the premises are destroyed, etc. Let's hope none of those things happen!

But there are certain other things that quite commonly extinguish an offer, even within the time frame. For example, you can almost always withdraw your offer, even during the time period that you gave the sellers to accept. This can get a bit tricky, however. The first rule is that you cannot withdraw the offer during the time period if the offer was complex and required the sellers to expend effort or money in determining whether or not to accept it, and the sellers have already begun to do so. For example, perhaps the sellers were facing complex tax issues involving the sale and had to consult an accountant. It's not fair to pull the rug out from under them after they start working on it. For an ordinary sale of a house, this hardly ever applies, but I've run into it a few times.

The second rule is that you cannot withdraw the offer during the stated time period if you accepted money from the sellers in exchange for an agreement to leave it open. A line that says "offer to remain open for 30 days if the sellers give the buyer $100" is enforceable assuming the sellers tender the $100. It is enforceable because you have really created an option. The sellers have an option to sell you the property at the state price for the 30 days, and you accepted their payment in exchange for it.

Under normal circumstances, though, the offeror can withdraw the offer any time, even if the offer states that it remains open for a period of time. However, you cannot withdraw the offer once the other side has accepted it and their acceptance has been communicated to you. Note that you have until you learn that they have accepted it. Even if they have already signed it, you can withdraw if you have not been told yet that they did so.

Your offer is also extinguished if the sellers reject it. Rejection of an offer extinguishes the offer. That's an absolute statement with no exceptions. The sellers cannot reject your offer, then later have a change of heart and decide to accept it. (Well, they can, but then their actions really constitute an offer to sell — a completely new offer — which you have no obligation to accept. Your offer died when the sellers rejected it.)

Sometimes, however, the sellers will make a counteroffer instead of a rejection. Usually, this also extinguishes your original offer. The reason is clear if you think of what a counteroffer is.

What the sellers are saying by making a counteroffer is "no, but here is what we *will* take." Notice the "no" in the preceding sentence. Once the sellers say "no," it is a rejection of your offer. All a counteroffer is (usually) is a rejection of the offer, coupled with a new offer back. The sellers are now offering to you. Your original roles of offeror and offeree have been reversed.

Now the ball is in your court. The sellers can put whatever they want into the counteroffer, including time limits. You can accept, reject, or counter again. This can go on for some time. I've had sales where I wrote so many offers and counteroffers that the file got too thick to get into one file folder. Don't worry about it. I always said "as long as the buyer and seller are still talking, I'll find the time to drive back and forth with their offers — there's a commission in this somewhere." I just had to find it. And I almost always did.

Notice that each time a counteroffer is made, the other party's preceding offer is usually extinguished. However, it doesn't have to be that way. An outright rejection always extinguishes an offer, but it's possible to make a counteroffer without extinguishing the original offer. The sellers just have to say that's what they're doing, and then they can keep the original offer to consider. For example, suppose you offer $100,000 and agree to leave the offer open for 30 days. The sellers respond by saying "we'll continue to consider your offer for the remaining time, but in case you want to stop worrying that we might sell to someone else in the meantime, we'll sell to you right now for $110,000." Of course, this rarely happens in residential sales, but I just thought I would toss it in just in case. (See how involved contract law can get? Aren't you glad you're not a lawyer?)

One final note about offers — when the other side accepts an offer, the acceptance must be a 100% acceptance of the offer as stated, or it constitutes a counteroffer. The slightest change in the original offer becomes a counteroffer. The sellers might accept your offer but stipulate that the closing date be one day earlier. That's a counteroffer. You have no obligation to accept it. Of course, something as trivial as that is probably something you'd want to go ahead and agree to, but it's your decision.

These days there is almost always a counteroffer because the sellers and their agent think of things the buyers and their agent forgot about. Or sometimes they just want to clarify the language of the contract. Some agents call these "technical counteroffers," meaning they are trivial issues not really affecting the main intent. But no matter how trivial, in the eyes of the law they are still counteroffers and the original offeror has no obligation to accept them.

Unenforceability

Even when a contract appears to have been formed (offer made and properly accepted) there are a handful of things that can render the contract unenforceable after the fact. These don't occur often, but here's a list of common ones anyway —

• Mutual mistake of fact — Both of you were laboring under a misapprehension of the facts. E.g., the seller thought the property boundary was in a certain place, so did you, but later you discover you were both mistaken. Contract can be set aside by the party damaged by the error. (See also fraud and misrepresentation below.)

• Incompetence (lack of legal capacity) — If you're under 18, or if you are mentally incompetent, you may set aside any contract you enter into within a reasonable time after gaining competence. Note: If buying property owned by a corporation, the corporation cannot be held to the contract unless it was signed on behalf of the corporation by someone authorized to sign by the board of directors. To be sure the person signing is authorized, the usual practice is to have the president and secretary sign a corporate resolution stating that the board of directors gave their authority.

• Impossibility — A contract is rendered unenforceable on either party if it becomes impossible to perform. The classic example is an earnest money agreement for the sale of a house. Both parties have signed it and it is a binding contract. Prior to closing the house burns to the ground. Kind of tough for the seller to deliver the goods now, isn't it? The contract is no longer enforceable due to impossibility. Impossibility generally has to be due to an act of God, not because one of the parties cannot perform due to financial difficulties.

• Mutual cancellation or rescission — You can mutually agree to undo anything.

- Bankruptcy — (Let's hope it's the seller, not you!) If the seller files a bankruptcy after agreeing to sell you the property, the whole transaction is thrown into the bankruptcy court. You'll have to wait until the court makes a final ruling before you can consummate the transaction. Most standard earnest money forms have a clause allowing you to bail out if that happens — after all, it could take six months or longer before the bankruptcy hearing.

Fraud and misrepresentation

Fraud and misrepresentation also cause a contract to become unenforceable. Fraud is a deliberate lie, or deliberate withholding of the truth when the party had a duty to disclose it, causing damage to the other party. To constitute fraud the party making the representation must have known the truth, the other party must have acted on it to his or her detriment, and must have had a right to rely on the representation. Statute of limitations is two years from discovery of the truth in Oregon, but may be as long as three years in Washington. Fraud not only allows the damaged party to set aside the contract or seek damages, but is also a criminal act.

Misrepresentation is a false statement, or failure to state a fact when the party had a duty to do so, but where the party did not know the truth. The damaged party may set aside the contract. Statute of limitations is two years from discovery. Misrepresentation allows the damaged party to set aside the contract, or sometimes seek damages, but is not a criminal matter.

Misrepresentation is either negligent or innocent. Negligent misrepresentation means the party could have checked the facts, but failed to do so, and therefore made false statement or failed to disclose when he or she had a duty to do so.

Innocent misrepresentation is when the party did check, the source is one that should be considered reliable, but the party made a false statement or failed to disclose to you because the source was incorrect. For example, suppose the sellers rely upon their understanding of the property boundaries, which are what was represented to them when they bought the property. Unfortunately, the sellers have been laboring under a delusion all these years, and they pass on to you the incorrect information. Whether

Chapter 8, The Large Print Giveth and the Fine Print Taketh Away

negligent or innocent, one of your remedies is the same — you can set aside the contract and ask for your money back. If negligent, you may ask for damages instead of setting the contract aside.

In real estate sales by far the most common problem is negligent misrepresentation of the condition of the property. Occasionally there are problems with property boundaries, and once in a while there are issues involving water rights or zoning (usually only in vacant land sales), but the biggest problem by far is the condition of the improvements.

Failing to disclose these issues has become such a problem that both Oregon and Washington require the seller to make a disclosure of the condition of the property to buyers of residential property (one to four units only). Both states exempt certain transactions such as sales of brand-new residences, transfers by gift or inheritance, etc.

Oregon adds a couple of exemptions from the disclosure requirements —

- A property not to be occupied by the buyer or the buyer's family
- A property that has never been occupied by the seller

In Oregon, if exempt, the seller need do nothing. If not exempt, the seller must deliver to anyone making an offer on the property either a disclosure form specified by Oregon statute (see Appendix A), or a disclaimer that the seller makes no warranties or representations and the buyer takes the property as is.

If the seller gives the buyer the disclaimer it must state that the buyer has seven days to revoke the offer. If the seller gives the buyer the disclosure form, then the buyer has five days to revoke the offer. If the seller does neither, then the buyer may revoke any time up till closing. If the buyer revokes, regardless of whether under the disclosure, the disclaimer, or neither, the buyer is entitled to a refund of everything the buyer paid toward the purchase price. Once the buyer closes, however, all rights to revoke the offer expire, regardless of whether the seller disclosed, disclaimed, or did neither.

Washington's disclosure law has no extra exemptions. Further, there is no provision for a disclaimer form. The sellers must give the buyer the disclosure form required by Washington law (see Appendix A). The buyer has three business days after receipt of the disclosure form to cancel the transaction, in which case the buyer is entitled to a refund of any deposits or other consideration paid. If the sellers refuse to give the buyer the disclosure form, then the buyer may cancel the transaction any time up to closing. As in Oregon, once the sale closes the buyer has no further right to cancel the transaction.

The problem is, what if the sellers give you a disclosure statement that lists no problems with the property. After you move in you discover a defect. Now what?

The answer is, "it depends." First, is the problem serious enough to do something about it. The law calls such an issue a "material fact." A small tear in the wallpaper that was hidden behind the couch is probably not a material fact. A broken furnace undoubtedly is. It's a material fact if an ordinary buyer would have offered different terms, a different price, or not have bought at all if he or she had known the truth. Unless it is a material fact, you have no grounds for a suit.

Secondly, it has to be something which the sellers knew, or could or should have known. This gets trickier. Of course, the sellers will say they didn't know. But if the furnace doesn't work, how could they not know? And even if they swear they didn't know, you will say "but you certainly should have known." Not necessarily. What if the seller is a bank that took the property in as a foreclosure. They have never lived there. They have never rented it to a tenant. The point is that whether the sellers could have or should have known depends on the situation. At least, that's the way the courts will look at it. Whether the sellers could or should have known is up to the court. Each case is decided on its own individual merits.

And the third issue is that the defect must have been "latent." Latent means that it was hidden from view during a normal inspection. Bad wiring inside the walls would be latent, for example. But dry rot around the basement window sills which are plainly visible when walking around the property is not latent. Again, the law applies different standards to different situations. If you are blind, for example, everything is latent.

Assuming you have discovered a material latent defect, then you have cause to complain to the seller. Depending on which state you are in, the law allows you two or three years from discovery of the defect to file suit. Hopefully it can be negotiated without the need for a suit, but every day more and more such suits are filed.

The best way to avoid these problems is to order an inspection of the property. Unfortunately, inspection services cannot usually be held liable if they miss something. The only real benefit is that they are professionals, so they know what to look for, plus they have special tools and equipment to test various components of the house. Also, they will go into places where there may be crawly things that you and I don't want to know about.

Bear in mind that there are inspections and there are inspections. The inspection agreement will stipulate what the inspector is to look for. For example, unless it says otherwise, the inspection order does not obligate the inspector to look for pest infestation. You need to be clear about what the inspector is going to inspect, and be comfortable with the decision.

I should also mention that inspections are not insurance. If you want insurance there are homeowner warranty policies available. Personally I love it when the buyer gets such a policy because it means I won't be getting any irate phone calls from the buyer after the sale is closed. Of course, you want the seller to pay for it, something to consider in your negotiations.

On occasion we run into sellers who are genuinely dishonest. Once I had a seller remove the expensive oak cabinets from the kitchen and replace them with vinyl-clad pasteboard cabinets just before closing. I have heard other agents tell stories of sellers removing even the bathtub and other fixtures. Someday I'm sure a buyer is going to go to move in and discover the sellers decided just to take the whole darn house.

How do we deal with this? Nowadays it is common for the buyer to have the right to a "last minute walk-through." This is commonly done a day or two before closing. It's not a perfect solution, as the sellers still have time to rip things off. Still, at least it allows the buyer to see that the sellers have continued to keep the grounds maintained and other items are still OK. A better solution is for the listing agent to take lots of pictures of the interior of the house at the time of taking the listing. These photographs can be subpoenaed if necessary. Just knowing that there exists evidence of what was in the house is usually enough to stop larcenous sellers from trying to pull a fast one.

Contingencies

Real estate agents use the word "contingencies," but lawyers call them "conditions." It doesn't matter — the courts accept both terms as synonyms. Lawyers even get carried away with categorizing them, but that doesn't really matter either. If there is a contingency in the contract and it is not met, the contract is not enforceable on the party in whose favor the contingency is stated.

The most common contingency in an earnest money agreement is the financing. Assuming you have to get final loan approval in order to buy the house, your earnest money agreement will state the kind of loan you are to get, that you will apply for it within a stated time period and use your best efforts to obtain it, but if you cannot get it you are released from the contract and your earnest money is to be refunded. If it did not state this, and if the loan could not be obtained, then you would be obligated to pay cash. And if you failed to do so, your earnest money would be forfeit. Pretty important contingency, eh?

There are tons of other common contingencies in earnest money agreements. Real estate agents try to avoid contingencies as much as possible, and you should too. The cleaner your offer, the better chance of getting it accepted. The financing contingency is so common, however, that people don't even think of it as a contingency. And sellers will generally go along with anything where they can see you have a valid reason for it.

But if it looks like you're using a contingency as a weasel clause, expect a negative reaction. Once I had an investor insist on making an offer contingent on the approval of his brother. I asked why the brother's approval was important. I expected him to say something like the brother was putting up part of the money, or the brother was an expert in building and construction — some legitimate reason why the buyer wanted his brother to approve the purchase. The investor's response was that he could use the brother's disapproval to bail out of the deal any time he wanted to. Since the approval of the brother had no limitations, all the investor had to do was tell his brother to refuse to approve the deal. Since I was acting as a seller's agent in that transaction, I had to tell the seller what the buyer had told me, whereupon the seller refused to have anything further to do with the buyer.

Some additional common contingencies —
- Subject to the approval of other professionals (accountant, attorney, etc.)
- Subject to inspection (very common today)
- Subject to sale of another property (to be avoided — sellers will usually refuse such offers, meaning you will have to pay full price to get them to take it)
- Subject to someone else (usually relatives) agreeing to a gift of the down payment
- Subject to satisfactory interior inspection (common in properties which are currently rented because you have to give the tenants 24-hours' notice to go inside)
- Subject to inspection of the yard during the daylight (very common during northwest winter months)

- Subject to approval of co-buyer (e.g., your spouse is out of town when you make the offer). Note: In Oregon either spouse can buy the property and state that title is to be in both names or either name alone. In Washington, both must sign in order to buy.

Contingencies are also commonly used to avoid a misrepresentation. Buyers are always asking specifics about the property and sometimes the seller's agent doesn't know the answer. Rather than hazard a guess, which the buyer might claim was a misrepresentation if it turns out to be untrue, the seller's agent might suggest that you make your offer subject to verification of the issue that is bothering you. Now, the worst that can happen is that the problem turns out as you feared, you ask for your money back, and the transaction falls through. Having a sale fail to close is better than one which closes and results in a lawsuit later.

Remedies

If the seller agrees to the contract and later refuses to go through with it, the buyer's usual remedy is either damages or a special remedy called "specific performance." Specific performance is asking the court to order the other party to perform the contract as agreed. To claim damages you have to demonstrate the amount you were damaged. In contract law you cannot get punitive damages, only the amount you were actually out, plus costs. (When you read in the paper about multi-million dollar damage awards, it is almost always punitive damages, not actual damages.) Actual damages could be expenses such as appraisal and loan fees, inspection fees, and other charges that you cannot recover. Of course, you are also entitled to a refund of your earnest money.

If the buyer defaults, the sellers' remedies are a bit more complicated. The sellers can sue the buyer for specific performance too, asking the court to order the buyer to perform. Or the sellers can sue for damages. But again, the sellers can only get the actual damages, not punitive damages. The sellers may be hard-pressed to come up with significant real damages sustained due to the buyer backing out wrongfully.

However, the most commonly used seller remedy is to declare that the earnest money is forfeit. This is where it depends on the exact wording of the contract. Although the law gives the seller all three remedies, the most commonly used residential earnest money agreement in Oregon (a form jointly created by the Oregon Association of Realtors®, and the local boards of Portland and Eugene) allows the seller only to declare a forfeiture of all the earnest money.

In Washington there are two forms in common use. One of these (created by the Washington Association of Realtors®) provides the seller with the sole remedy of declaring a forfeiture of the earnest money, but limits the amount to 5% of the sales price, the buyer being entitled to a refund of any surplus. The other, created by the Northwest Multiple Listing Service (of the Seattle area, but the form is in general use throughout the state) provides for either a forfeiture of the earnest money (up to 5% of the sales price) or the other remedies as well. There are other forms used in Washington too, which may allow the seller only forfeiture of the earnest money or all of the standard remedies. The only way to be sure is to read the form before signing.

Earnest money agreements (purchase agreements)

The earnest money agreement is really two documents in one. It is a receipt for the actual earnest money, and it is a contract specifying the terms of the sale. Thus it is sometimes called the "purchase agreement" or "purchase and sale agreement" and sometimes the "earnest money agreement," "earnest money receipt," or similar terms. I have even heard it called a "binder." Hereafter, I'll just call it the "earnest money agreement," since that is probably the most commonly used term throughout the northwest.

Every sale involves an earnest money agreement. When you make an offer to buy, your agent will fill out an earnest money agreement for you to sign in order to make your formal offer. Your agent will sign it too and give you a copy of it, because it also functions as a receipt for the earnest money you are giving your agent to hold. When the sellers accept your offer they will sign the earnest money agreement as well. Then your agent will bring you back a copy of it with the sellers' signatures on it, as evidence of the final agreement. Of course, sometimes counteroffers get interjected in the middle of this scenario, but that's at least how the transaction works in its simplest configuration.

One of the things that will be specified in the earnest money agreement is the amount of earnest money, of course. This will be credited to you at closing, so there is no reason not to make it a substantial amount. The larger the earnest money deposit, the more impressive your offer. When trying to buy a house for a lowball price by offering all cash, I have had clients write an earnest money check for the entire purchase price. When I presented the offer, the sellers were peering at the check in my hand trying to count the number of zeros on it.

If you don't want to give a check for the earnest money, you can use a note. In fact, anything can be used as earnest money — even another piece of real estate, a car — anything that you want to pledge. However, nothing impresses the seller like a personal check, and for a substantial amount.

You need not worry about security. All agents are required to deposit earnest money given to them into a clients' trust account (in Washington they are very commonly called "escrow accounts," but the function is the same). These accounts are audited by the state licensing agency. Every agent knows that even the slightest misuse of funds is grounds for immediately license revocation. You can give the deposit to an agent with as much confidence as you would to an attorney or any other professional.

If you are in Oregon you can ask the agent to deposit the funds to an interest-bearing account, although the time period involved is so short that it is usually more trouble than it is worth. Oregon license law allows it to be held in the trust account of the buyer's agent, of the seller's agent, or of a neutral escrow company. While it would probably be slightly better if it were in the trust account of your own agent, the common practice is to use a neutral escrow company, and it isn't probably worth the argument to do otherwise. After all, if the transaction falls through and you are entitled to a refund of it, whoever is holding it is required by state law to make the refund, regardless of who that happens to be.

Washington buyers cannot get interest on their earnest money unless it is at least $10,000 and you ask the agent to put it in a separate interest-bearing account. Washington license law requires agents to deposit all funds under $10,000 into a pooled interest-bearing account on which the interest will be paid to the state housing trust fund (for homeless housing) and a portion to the licensing agency (to further education of real estate agents).

Although the language of every earnest money form will be slightly different, at some point there will be a section describing the title to the property you are to receive. It will say that you are to receive "marketable title" (or the synonym, "insurable title"). Marketable title means that the property is free and clear of financial encumbrances, but not necessarily completely free of other burdens. This can get a bit tricky. For example, an easement across the property is a burden on the title. Normally you don't have to agree to take the title subject to the easement. But if it is an easement for utilities which benefit the property, this is considered acceptable within the definition of "marketable title" — so no special agreement is needed.

How do you know whether the property is subject to financial or other encumbrances? The answer is, you don't. That's what title insurance companies are for. They research the history of the title and issue you a title insurance policy. Normally, the seller pays the premium, although who pays for it (like just about any other expense) is negotiable.

The problem is that the title insurance company cannot issue you a title insurance policy insuring that you are in title until you are, in fact, in title. That means the sellers have to give you the deed. And the sellers won't want to give you the deed until they have the cash. And you won't want to give them the cash until you get title insurance. This goes around and around and it looks as though the transaction is never going to close.

The solution is the "preliminary title report." This is not insurance; it's just the title insurance company's statement that they are willing to issue the policy. The terms of the earnest money agreement state that you agree to close and give the sellers the cash based on the preliminary title report, assuming it says the title insurance company will issue a policy with marketable title. Then, a few days after closing, you will receive the actual policy in the mail.

I should make a special note about where you get title insurance. Every county in the northwest is served by several competing title insurance companies. The decision as to which company to use is the buyer's, if you are financing the property. This is because of the federal Real Estate Settlement Procedures Act, which prohibits anyone in the transaction from requiring the buyer to obtain any needed service from any particular provider of the service. The purpose is to encourage the buyer to shop for the best price. Of course, title insurance rates are virtually the same from one company to the next, so it doesn't make a lot of difference.

Another important, but confusing, part of the earnest money agreement is the section that deals with dates when things are supposed to happen. It will help if you bear in mind that there are always three dates in every transaction —
- Closing date — the date everything is finalized
- Possession date — the date you are entitled to move in
- Prorate date — the date as of which the buyer and the seller apportion the ongoing expenses of the property between them, e.g., the property taxes.

All three of these could be stipulated to be the same date. Or any two can be the same and the third a different date. Or all three can be different. And any of them can be before or after any of the others. It just depends on what you and the seller want to agree to.

It is typical to give possession the day after closing, but sometimes the sellers want more time to move and don't want to start packing until they know it is closed. If they ask for too much time, however, they are living in your house, so it's appropriate to object. You can ask for rent, although this causes a psychological problem ("we're not paying rent for our own house!"). Of course, it isn't their house any more, but you see the psychology. Better to negotiate around it some other way.

The opposite of this is also possible — the buyers want to move in before closing. This is always inadvisable. Nevertheless, it happens from time to time. You gave notice to your landlord that you would be out by the end of the month, but closing becomes unavoidably delayed. If you can renegotiate with your landlord, that is a better solution. But if the landlord has rerented the place to a new tenant and they are set to move in, you may have little choice but to ask the sellers to let you move in before closing.

The prorate date is usually stated as either the same as the possession date or the closing date. In other words, you should be responsible for the bills of the property either from the time it is yours (closing) or the time you move in (possession). Whichever you specify is what the closing agent will use when apportioning how many dollars to charge or credit each side for the ongoing expenses of the property.

What are you buying, anyway?

One of the biggest trouble areas in real estate transactions is what's included with the property and what's not. If I had a dollar for every time a buyer and a seller got into an argument about this, I'd be really, really rich.

First, a little terminology. Unless the agreement says otherwise, all you're buying is the real estate. Unfortunately, most people have a slightly incorrect notion of what this is. Most people think "if it's attached, it's real estate." This is not completely accurate. Many items can be considered part of the real estate, even if not attached — e.g., the remote control for the garage door opener. Even the house keys are part of the real estate, and they sure aren't attached.

And there are even more items that can be attached and yet not considered part of the real estate. The exact laws dealing with this are complex. But there is one thing that saves us from having to go to law school just to buy a house. The law says that, regardless of whether the item would normally be considered part of the real estate or not, if the parties specifically agree that it is or is not part of the real estate, then that's the way it is. In other words, if there is any doubt about the item, just mention it one way or the other in the earnest money agreement and whatever the law would normally say about this item generally becomes irrelevant.

The problem is spotting the questionable items. Because there are certain items that are perennial problem areas, every standard earnest money form has a list printed right in the form. And since this list may not include everything the parties need to mention for their specific transaction, there is a blank where you can specify added items that are to be included, and another blank where you can list things normally considered part of the real estate that you are willing to let the sellers remove and take with them. Items that are not real estate but which are to be included anyway are called "inclusions"; and items of real estate that the seller may remove are called "exclusions."

If you have any question about whether an item is automatically included, for heavens sake, speak up! It is generally your agent's job to know what is included and what is not included. Of course, even an attorney skilled in real estate law may not know the answer to every issue. If your agent says he or she does not know for sure if the object you ask about is normally considered part of the real estate, fair enough. Just remember, if there is any doubt about whether something is part of the real estate, stipulate it in the earnest money agreement. The courts generally follow what the contract says unless it says nothing.

Now that you have some idea of the terms of a typical earnest money agreement, you need to get your real estate agent to give you a blank copy of the form he or she will use to write up your offer when you find the house you want to buy. Study it over and familiarize yourself with it a bit. If there is anything that you don't understand, you can mark it and ask your agent to explain it to you next time you meet. This will give you something to talk about in the car on the way to look at properties, and will save time when it comes to actually making the offer.

Just to amuse you, on the following page is an example of an earnest money agreement we used to use when I was selling real estate many years ago. It was just a half-page long. Compare it to the sample your agent gives you. Be prepared for a shock! And the interesting thing is, I had fewer problems closing transactions based on that form than I do on the forms we use today.

A little vocabulary

When you get the copy of the earnest money agreement from your agent, the following additional terminology may help you understand it —

- Statutory warranty deed — The deed form that offers the buyer the best protection.
- Foreign Investment in Real Property Tax Act — A federal law that requires the closing agent to withhold income taxes from the sales proceeds if the seller is a foreigner. Does not affect the buyer; only the seller and the closing agent.
- Recording — For the protection of the buyer, the seller's deed must be recorded. Otherwise, the seller could fraudulently sell the property to someone else. If the second party records his or her deed first, you lose the title. First to record is first in right. The lender's loan documents must also be recorded, as well as a statement for the seller's old lender that the loan is paid in full. The closing agent takes care of this.
- Assignment — Means putting someone else in your shoes in a contract. Most earnest money forms allow the sellers to assign at will, because it doesn't matter to the buyer if they do. But if the buyers assign, the new buyer may not be able to qualify

Date _____, City _____, State _____,
I/we _____ agree to purchase for the sum of $ _____
the following described real property in _____ County, State of _____,
subject to obtaining a _____ loan in the amount of $ _____. I/we agree
to pay all costs associated with said loan. Earnest money, to be credited to buyer(s) at closing is herewith
deposited in the amount of $ _____ in the form of (check)(cash)(note).
Closing to be as soon as financing can be arranged and documents prepared. Prorates to be as of closing
date. Possession to be _____ days after closing.
Seller to provide buyer(s) with standard form title insurance within a reasonable time after closing at seller's expense. Buyer and seller to prorate the expenses for taxes, insurance, assumed debt and rent, if any, as of possession date.
The following items are included with the property _____. Seller
may remove the following items from the property _____.

_____ _____
Buyer   Buyer
Broker by _____ Agent
I/we agree to sell the property on the above terms and to pay the broker above a commission of
$ _____ for services in this transaction.

_____ _____
Seller   Seller

financially, so most forms prohibit the buyer from assigning without the seller's permission.

- Escrow — A closing agent. Usually a department of a title insurance company, but may also be an independent company. Transactions in Oregon are almost always closed in escrow. In Washington many transactions are closed by the banks where the sale is financed. The closing agent is a neutral agent of the buyer and seller.
- Standard form title insurance — The kind of policy that sellers typically provide for buyers. The lender will also require a title insurance policy to insure that they have a good and valid lien on the property and they will demand the extended coverage policy. The buyer is normally expected to pay the premium for the lender's policy, but it is customary for the seller to pay the premium for the buyer's standard form policy. If you are purchasing new construction or a property that has been substantially renovated within the past couple of months, you may ask for a buyer's extended coverage policy. The extended coverage policy covers construction liens, which are excluded from the coverage of a standard form policy. The seller may balk at paying the higher premium required, however.
- Time is of the essence — A commonly misunderstood term — does not mean you have to hurry up. It means any dates in the contract are for real. Without this clause you'd have to notify the other side of their failure to perform by a due date before you could declare them to be in default.
- Fixture — Something attached to the real estate and now considered to be part of it — e.g., the furnace, a drop in range, etc.
- Lien — A financial encumbrance on the property, e.g., a mortgage. Property taxes are also a lien. Anything which allows the lienholder to foreclose in order to enforce collection of a financial obligation is a lien.
- Trust deed — A modern replacement for a mortgage. Today we still say "mortgage loan" but the actual document is almost always a trust deed. The trust deed creates a lien on the property in favor of the lender and allows the lender to foreclose to enforce collection, if necessary. Lenders prefer trust deeds to mortgages because they are faster and cheaper to foreclose on.

Options and lease options

First a little terminology so we know what we're talking about. An option is generally thought of by the public as an option to buy, but actually it can work the other way too — if you agree to buy a property at a certain price any time the seller wants to sell it to you, you have given the seller an option to sell. Any contract can make performance by the other side optional, in which case it is an option to do whatever the contract provides for.

If the seller gives you an option to buy, then the seller is the optionor and you are the optionee. To be valid, an option must state a consideration, although the amount can be a nominal amount if the parties agree. An option must also be in writing, be signed by the optionor, and contain a legal description of the property.

The key to understanding an option to buy is that it is really just an earnest money agreement where the buyer's performance is optional. In fact, you could create an option just by filling out a standard earnest money agreement and then writing in the margin a statement to the effect that the buyer's performance is optional.

Unless otherwise stated, the presumption is that only the agreement to perform must be made firm within the time period of the option. In other words, if you have an option to buy for 90 days, you are allowed a reasonable period to close the transaction as long as you state your intention to do so within the 90 days. Once you state that you will perform, then you are obligated to perform.

The important thing to remember about options to buy is that they must state all the terms of the sale the same as an earnest money agreement. Otherwise you will have endless arguments with the seller over who is to pay the different fees, when the closing and possession dates are to be, what is included with the real estate, and so on. Earnest money agreement forms are engineered with blanks to fill in which cover all those details. An option form needs to be equally detailed.

Lease options

Lease options are very popular with buyers who have little or no money. Unfortunately, it is a rare buyer who understands how they work. Once the buyer discovers how lease-options are typically structured, their interest fades quickly.

First, the legalities. A lease option is nothing more than a lease and an option written together. The sellers lease you the property, and in the same breath give you an option to buy it. For information about how the option part works, see above.

Now let's get to the problems. Buyers seem to think that the sellers are just going to credit them with all their rent toward the down payment. No sellers in their right mind are going to do this. The sellers are going to feel that, as long as they are in title, they are entitled to all the rent the same as any landlord. After all, they have expenses to pay, and they have an investment they are entitled to receive a return on.

Therefore, it is customary to charge higher rent than otherwise, and give credit toward the down payment for only a small portion of it. This still can be a valid way to buy a house, but it certainly isn't as appealing as most buyers think it's going to be.

Then there are other difficulties. Sellers willing to lease-option their properties usually do so because they perceive it as a way to get a much higher sales price. The reality is that you almost always pay a very high price for the property when you buy on a lease option.

Another problem is that real estate agents practically never deal with options. The reason is simple practicality. The agent needs some serious cash flow somewhere in the transaction to siphon a commission out of. When you buy a house with outside financing, the seller is cashed out, so there is plenty of cash. Even when you buy on an owner contract, you usually make a down payment big enough to cover the commission without the sellers having to dig in their pockets to pay their agent.

But with a lease-option, all that changes hands is the first month's rent and a deposit. Agents would have to ask the sellers to pay the remainder of the commission out of their pockets. This isn't usually practical. And over 90% of all properties for sale are listed with real estate agents. The few that are available for lease-option are hard to find and not generally choice properties.

And the clincher is that, given today's financing options, there is really little need to lease-option a property anyway. Today you can get 100% financing even on conventional loans. There is just no need to bother with a lease-option.

Knowing something about contracts can be very helpful in making a good buy. It's important to understand the psychology of contract negotiations, but you also have to know what is possible before you can know what to ask for. And knowing how the offer and acceptance process works can increase your odds too.

The minute you read something you can't understand, you can almost be sure it was drawn up by a lawyer.
WILL ROGERS

Chapter 9

An Escrow Is Not a Large Noisy Bird

Eventually your real estate purchase must be finalized. After weeks (sometimes months) of pleading with lenders, arranging inspections, and mostly sitting around waiting, the transaction will be ready to close.

The problem now is that the sellers don't trust you, and you don't trust the sellers much either. What if you gave the money to the sellers and they just took off? Trust me, it wouldn't be the first time.

The solution is to use a third party to handle the closing. In Oregon that is almost always an escrow agent. In Washington it is usually an escrow agent, but some sales are closed by the financial institution where the buyer obtains the financing. If so, the lender is acting as an escrow agent and has the same duties and functions.

Many escrow agents operate as independent companies. They must be licensed by the state and are subject to rigid rules regarding handling of documents and funds. After all, they frequently handle transactions involving millions of dollars. You will also find that all the title insurance companies offer an escrow service along with their title insurance business. It doesn't really matter whether you use an independent escrow company or the escrow service of a title insurance company, or if you close in the lender's office. All will be neutral and all will generally provide the same level of competence.

The best thing is to shop for the price, as escrow fees usually run to a couple hundred dollars or more. If you call around you can find prices that range from $150 or so to several hundred dollars. If you are financing the purchase with a third party loan (not carried by the seller), federal law gives you the option to decide where to close the transaction, so you may as well shop for the lowest price. Whatever you do, do not blindly follow the recommendation of your lender or anyone else involved in the transaction. This is one area where you can save a significant amount of money.

Note that agents are accustomed just to making this decision for their clients. Even your own buyer's agent is likely just to specify the closing agent he or she likes to use without asking if you have any objections. The law says the decision is yours, so use it. Call around to determine who will charge the least, then tell your agent that is where you want to close. Your agent may be surprised, but will have no choice but to follow your instructions.

Because the escrow agent is neutral, it is customary for the buyer and seller to split the fee. (Exception: If you are financing with a federal GI loan, the U.S. Department of Veterans Affairs does not allow the veteran to pay any part of an escrow fee. It's a dumb rule, but it's always been that way.)

It's important to remember that an escrow agent is a neutral, third party. Think of an escrow as a stakeholder. You give the down payment money to the escrow, the bank gives them the rest of the purchase price in the form of your loan proceeds, and the seller gives them the deed. When everyone has given the escrow everything they are supposed to, the escrow wraps it all up. The seller's deed to you is recorded to make it official that you are now the owner. The lender's mortgage is also recorded, making it official that you owe them the money. And then the escrow uses the loan proceeds and your down payment to write a check to the sellers for the amount due them.

That makes it sound pretty simple, doesn't it? Gosh, anyone could be an escrow closer, right? Well, there is considerably more detail to consider.

Usually the real estate agent handling the transaction does not open an escrow until the loan has been approved. After all, until then there is always the possibility that the transaction could fall through. No point in wasting the time and effort setting up the escrow until we're sure we're going to need it. Setting up the escrow can be done in a few minutes, so there is nothing to be gained by doing it ahead of time.

In Oregon real estate agents are allowed to take an earnest money check from a client, open an escrow with the escrow agent that will do the final closing, and deposit the check to the escrow immediately. This practice is common, especially in the metropolitan areas. Washington brokers, however, are required to maintain all clients' funds in their own trust accounts until needed for closing.

Escrow (closing) instructions

When all the contingencies have been met and the transaction is ready to close, the agents will transfer to the closing agent any funds they are still holding, plus copies of the earnest money agreement and any other documents that have been generated along the way. The escrow agent will review these documents and create "escrow instructions" for the parties to sign.

The escrow instructions are quite detailed, explaining exactly what you are instructing the escrow agent to do. For the buyer's side, it will say (among other matters) "give the sellers the money only after the sellers have delivered the deed and you have a preliminary title report showing that they really own the property."

Your lender will also be asked to sign escrow instructions. Their instructions will say "deposit this check for the loan proceeds for the buyer's credit only after the buyer has signed the enclosed loan documents and you have a preliminary title report showing that the lien will be good" (i.e., that the borrower will really own the house after closing).

And finally, the sellers will give the escrow instructions saying "here is the deed to the property; give it to the buyer when you have the money to pay us the amount of the purchase price."

Notice how these separate instructions all mesh neatly. Once everyone has done what they are supposed to do, the escrow can close the transaction.

Of course, once in a while there is a problem. If the instructions from one of the parties don't mesh with the instructions from another party, the escrow is deadlocked. The instructions have to create a way that the escrow can satisfy all instructions simultaneously. If not, the transaction cannot be closed until one or more parties modifies his or her instructions to make it work. Note: Escrows are not allowed to negotiate. To negotiate would require that they get a real estate agent's license. Therefore, if an escrow is ever deadlocked, they simply notify the parties of the problem and wait for them to resolve the matter. If they don't resolve the problem, the escrow politely returns all the funds and documents to the parties and tells them to come back when they have their act together.

When everything is ready to close, the usual practice is for the closing agent to call the real estate agents for the buyers and sellers and ask them to call their clients to make an appointment to come in and sign. Each party will come in separately. This avoids direct confrontation in case there are any last minute problems.

If you are using a buyer's agent, there is nothing wrong with asking your agent to accompany you to the closing. It is part of the service to which you are entitled. When I represent clients I do not always accompany them to the closing, but am always happy to do so if they ask. And if they are first-time buyers I always do, although if I am representing a veteran investor it is usually unnecessary. Even if I don't go to the closing with my client, I always stop by and review the documents first to make sure everything is as it is supposed to be.

Closing agents usually have preprinted escrow instruction forms for the parties to sign. Most use a "joint" form for the buyer and seller to sign. The lender's instructions are usually dictated by the lender, so the lender includes them with the check for the loan proceeds. Unlike earnest money agreements, there are no standard closing instruction forms; each closing agent will have their own printed up. On the following pages you will find a sample joint escrow instruction form that is typical of what you will encounter when you go to your own closing.

Joint Escrow Instructions

To: _____ [Name of closing agent]

Seller deposits with you an executed statutory warranty deed showing purchaser as grantee, and authorizes delivery to purchaser when you hold for seller's account the sum of _____ [Purchase price], plus and minus credits and charges as set forth herein.

Seller authorizes you to pay off the following existing encumbrances [list seller's old loans and amounts due, plus any other obligations of seller which are a lien on the property].

_____

_____

Purchaser approves the form of seller's statutory warranty deed above referenced.

Purchaser deposits with you an executed note and trust deed together with loan documents provided by _____ [Name of buyer's lender]. Purchaser will deposit additional sums as are necessary to cover the amount of the purchase price plus purchaser's costs and less purchaser's credits and loan proceeds. You are authorized to release these funds to the seller and other parties when you hold for purchaser the executed deed from the seller and title insurance in favor of purchaser in the amount of the purchase price showing marketable title.

You are authorized to prepare a bill of sale for seller's signature transferring to buyer title to any personal property included in this transaction.

You are authorized to prorate property taxes between purchaser and seller as of _____ [Prorate date].

We approve the tentative closing statement attached hereto showing which party will be charged and credited for the expenses involved in this transaction.

When all parts of this agreement have been complied with by the parties hereto, you are authorized to record any deeds, mortgages, trust deeds or contracts on behalf of the parties thereto. The parties understand that lenders frequently require their mortgages or trust deeds to be recorded prior to the close of the transaction and you are authorized to do so.

If you cannot comply with these instructions by _____ [cutoff date], to be referred to as the final cutoff date, you are instructed to return all documents and funds to the parties who originally delivered them to you upon written demand by the party.

You are authorized to furnish real estate agents of buyer and seller with copies of the final closing statement.

Closing agent assumes no liability for determining the nationality or foreign status of any seller in this transaction. Closing agent is not liable for collection or withholding of income taxes due under

Sections 1445 and 6039C of the Internal Revenue Code and regulations thereunder. Closing agent reserves the right to take any action required by said laws and regulations without further instructions from the parties to this escrow.

All funds received in this escrow shall be maintained in a general escrow account maintained by closing agent at a national or state chartered bank in this state without interest to the buyer or seller. The parties agree that this transaction will be closed only after any funds deposited by the parties are collected funds on deposit in said account.

In the event of dispute between the parties to this escrow, closing agent shall hold the funds and documents pending resolution of the dispute. If resolution is not forthcoming by the final cutoff date above referenced, closing agent shall, at option of closing agent, 1) return the funds and documents to the parties who originally deposited them and consider this escrow closed or, 2) join or commence a court action to determine the rights of the parties and deposit the funds and documents with the court.

In any suit or action brought by closing agent or any of the parties hereto, the prevailing party shall be entitled to recover the costs of said litigation.

The parties to this agreement have been advised that closing agent is authorized under state law to close this transaction but is not licensed as an attorney and that no legal advice has been given by closing agent as to the legal effect of any of the documents involved the value of the property or the advisability of the transaction. The parties to this transaction further acknowledge that they closing agent has not discouraged them from seeking the advice of an attorney or any other professional regarding this transaction or any of the documents involved therein.

The buyer and seller agree that all contingencies in their original purchase or earnest money agreement have been met or, if not met, that they will settle such matters outside this escrow.

The parties have been advised that this transaction may require the seller to deliver certain disclosure statements to buyer, as required by state law. The parties agree that such disclosures, if not already made, will be made outside this escrow, and that closing agent shall not have any liability therewith.

Dated this _____ day of _____, _____

Buyer	Seller
Buyer	Seller

Who pays what

With a few exceptions, every expense of closing a transaction is negotiable between the buyer and the seller. Nevertheless, there are some things that are customary. You need to know what is considered standard practice so you can be sure no one is taking advantage of you and that you are not erroneously charged an expense that the other side is supposed to pay.

The basic idea is that each side should pay those expenses which make it possible for them to do the transaction, or which protect their interest. As we go through the rest of this, remember this little rule.

Today there is a nearly certain probability that your transaction will be closed pursuant to the rules created by the federal Real Estate Settlement Procedures Act (RESPA). RESPA was created in 1974 to protect buyers of one- to four-family homes who finance them with outside lenders (seller-carried financing is exempt). "Settlement" is just a synonym for "closing." For example, at the end of the closing process you will be furnished with a "settlement statement," which is just as commonly called the "closing statement."

The main purpose of RESPA is to require disclosure of what you are being charged in such a way that you can shop for the service elsewhere and possibly obtain it more cheaply. To further this goal, RESPA prohibits anyone involved in the transaction from requiring that you secure a needed service from a particular provider of that service. For example, the title insurance company cannot require that you obtain closing services from a particular escrow company. You are free to shop.

Providers of services can refer you to other providers of services of course, and even recommend that you use their services. They just can't absolutely require it. And if a provider of a service refers you to another provider of a service, and the referring provider has an ownership interest in the other provider, that ownership interest must be disclosed. For example, there are occasionally real estate companies who operate their own escrow companies. If they refer you to their own escrow company, they must make a disclosure that they own the escrow company. Then it's your choice to decide if you think this constitutes a conflict of interest or might end up costing you higher fees than if you used a different escrow provider.

RESPA also prohibits kickbacks and unearned fees. For example, if a title insurance company were to pay a fee to a real estate agent for steering the agent's customers to them, this would be illegal. It would also be illegal if a lender charged you a fee for a service that was greater than it cost them to obtain the service. For example, suppose the appraiser charges the bank $300 for the appraisal, but the bank charges you $400, expecting to pocket the difference. RESPA makes such practices illegal.

RESPA affects everyone involved in the transaction. Even the sellers, for example, cannot require that you obtain a service you need from a particular provider. The sellers cannot require that you close at a certain escrow company, purchase title insurance from a particular title insurance company, have the property inspected by a specific inspection service, etc. All these are your choices. (Exception — if you don't have your own buyer's agent, the sellers can require that you make your offer through the sellers' agent.)

Although everyone in the transaction is affected by RESPA, the major burden of compliance falls on the lender. RESPA is primarily a disclosure law, and it is the lender who must make the initial disclosures. When you make loan application, the lender must provide you with a "good faith estimate" of the closing expenses on a Uniform Settlement Statement (HUD 1, see the sample on the next pages). The lender must also give you a copy of *Buying Your Home: Settlement Costs and Helpful Information*, a booklet written by HUD explaining the items on the Uniform Settlement Statement and encouraging you to shop for better prices on the services you need.

Once the transaction is ready to close the closing agent will have the final settlement statement ready. RESPA requires the closing agent to use the same form for the final statement, and you are entitled to review it at least one day before closing. Using the same form makes it easy for you to compare the items on the final closing statement with what is listed on the good faith estimate. I always recommend that buyers do this. At least half the time there is an error, usually in favor of the lender or the sellers.

The part of the Uniform Settlement Statement where you should be sure you are not incorrectly charged is lines 700 through 1305 on page 2 (see sample form on following pages). This is where the buyer's expenses are listed. The first part of the form (page 1) is just a summation (balance sheet). Most of the expense items on page 2 are self-explanatory, but a few need discussion. For example, lines 700-704 are for the real estate agent's commission. If your agreement with your agent requires you to pay a commission (also called a "brokerage fee"), you already know you are going to be charged so you can expect the amount to show up here.

Loan expenses (Section 800) are traditionally considered a buyer expense. After all, the loan makes it possible for you to buy the house (remember our little rule?). Of course, sometimes you can get the seller to agree to pay at least a portion of your loan expenses.

Whatever loan expenses you are supposed to pay will be listed here. When the lender makes the good faith estimate (at loan application) it will list all the fees. At least one of these you will pay in cash to the lender at the time of the loan application — the credit report fee — and there are occasionally others too, depending on the lender and the kind of loan you are getting. Be sure the closing agent didn't charge you for an expense that you already paid to the lender up front. I've encountered that error many times.

Section 900 is for prepaid items relating to the loan. One of the most confusing to borrowers is interest (line 901), and one where, if there is an error, it is always in favor of the lender. All real estate loans today (except bi-weekly loans) are structured so the payments fall due on the first. You have no choice in this. The reason is because the software used by loan servicers expects the payment on the first. And because loans are commonly sold, or at least servicing contracts are sold, the industry has had to standardize the due date.

The problem is that your purchase will undoubtedly fall somewhere in the middle of a month. Lenders want interest for each and every day the money is borrowed. And the software they

176   *Chapter 9, An Escrow Is Not a Noisy Black Bird*

A. Settlement Statement

U.S. Department of Housing and Urban Development

OMB Approval No. 2502-0265

B. Type of Loan

1. ☐ FHA	2. ☐ FmHA	3. ☐ Conv. Unins.	6. File Number:	7. Loan Number:	8. Mortgage Insurance Case Number:
4. ☐ VA	5. ☐ Conv. Ins.				

C. Note: This form is furnished to give you a statement of actual settlement costs. Amounts paid to and by the settlement agent are shown. Items marked "(p.o.c.)" were paid outside the closing; they are shown here for informational purposes and are not included in the totals.

D. Name & Address of Borrower:	E. Name & Address of Seller:	F. Name & Address of Lender:

G. Property Location:	H. Settlement Agent:	
	Place of Settlement:	I. Settlement Date:

J. Summary of Borrower's Transaction		K. Summary of Seller's Transaction	
100. Gross Amount Due From Borrower		**400. Gross Amount Due To Seller**	
101. Contract sales price		401. Contract sales price	
102. Personal property		402. Personal property	
103. Settlement charges to borrower (line 1400)		403.	
104.		404.	
105.		405.	
Adjustments for items paid by seller in advance		Adjustments for items paid by seller in advance	
106. City/town taxes to		406. City/town taxes to	
107. County taxes to		407. County taxes to	
108. Assessments to		408. Assessments to	
109.		409.	
110.		410.	
111.		411.	
112.		412.	
120. Gross Amount Due From Borrower		**420. Gross Amount Due To Seller**	
200. Amounts Paid By Or In Behalf Of Borrower		**500. Reductions In Amount Due To Seller**	
201. Deposit or earnest money		501. Excess deposit (see instructions)	

This is the front of the RESPA Good Faith Estimate and Settlement Statement. Lenders are required to give borrowers a copy with estimated closing costs at loan application. At least one day before closing the borrower is entitled to

Chapter 9, An Escrow Is Not a Noisy Black Bird

202. Principal amount of new loan(s)		502. Settlement charges to seller (line 1400)	
203. Existing loan(s) taken subject to		503. Existing loan(s) taken subject to	
204.		504. Payoff of first mortgage loan	
205.		505. Payoff of second mortgage loan	
206.		506.	
207.		507.	
208.		508.	
209.		509.	
Adjustments for items unpaid by seller		**Adjustments for items unpaid by seller**	
210. City/town taxes	to	510. City/town taxes	to
211. County taxes	to	511. County taxes	to
212. Assessments	to	512. Assessments	to
213.		513.	
214.		514.	
215.		515.	
216.		516.	
217.		517.	
218.		518.	
219.		519.	
220. Total Paid By/For Borrower		**520. Total Reduction Amount Due Seller**	
300. Cash At Settlement From/To Borrower		**600. Cash At Settlement To/From Seller**	
301. Gross Amount due from borrower (line 120)		601. Gross amount due to seller (line 420)	
302. Less amounts paid by/for borrower (line 220)	( )	602. Less reductions in amt. due seller (line 520)	( )
303. Cash ☐ From ☐ To Borrower		**603. Cash** ☐ To ☐ From Seller	

Section 5 of the Real Estate Settlement Procedures Act (RESPA) requires the following: • HUD must develop a Special Information Booklet to help persons borrowing money to finance the purchase of residential real estate to better understand the nature and costs of real estate settlement services; • Each lender must provide the booklet to all applicants from whom it receives or for whom it prepares a written application to borrow money to finance the purchase of residential real estate; • Lenders must prepare and distribute with the Booklet a Good Faith Estimate of the settlement costs that the borrower is likely to incur in connection with the settlement. These disclosures are manadatory.

Section 4(a) of RESPA mandates that HUD develop and prescribe this standard form to be used at the time of loan settlement to provide full disclosure of all charges imposed upon the borrower and seller. These are third party disclosures that are designed to provide the borrower with pertinent information during the settlement process in order to be a better shopper.

The Public Reporting Burden for this collection of information is estimated to average one hour per response, including the time for reviewing instructions, searching existing data sources, gathering and maintaining the data needed, and completing and reviewing the collection of information.

This agency may not collect this information, and you are not required to complete this form, unless it displays a currently valid OMB control number. The information requested does not lend itself to confidentiality.

Previous editions are obsolete   Page 1 of 2   form **HUD-1** (3/86) ref Handbook 4305.2

the final closing statement, which must be on the same form so borrowers can compare the estimate to the final figures. There are seldom errors on this side of the form because it is just a balance sheet.

L. Settlement Charges		Paid From Borrowers Funds at Settlement	Paid From Seller's Funds at Settlement
700. Total Sales/Broker's Commission based on price $ @ % =			
Division of Commission (line 700) as follows:			
701. $ to			
702. $ to			
703. Commission paid at Settlement			
704.			
800. Items Payable In Connection With Loan			
801. Loan Origination Fee	%		
802. Loan Discount	%		
803. Appraisal Fee	to		
804. Credit Report	to		
805. Lender's Inspection Fee			
806. Mortgage Insurance Application Fee to			
807. Assumption Fee			
808.			
809.			
810.			
811.			
900. Items Required By Lender To Be Paid In Advance			
901. Interest from to @ $ /day			
902. Mortgage Insurance Premium for months to			
903. Hazard Insurance Premium for years to			
904. years to			
905.			
1000. Reserves Deposited With Lender			
1001. Hazard insurance	months @ $ per month		
1002. Mortgage insurance	months @ $ per month		
1003. City property taxes	months @ $ per month		
1004. County property taxes	months @ $ per month		
1005. Annual assessments	months @ $ per month		
1006.	months @ $ per month		
1007.	months @ $ per month		
1008.	months @ $ per month		
1100. Title Charges			
1101. Settlement or closing fee	to		
1102. Abstract or title search	to		
1103. Title examination	to		
1104. Title insurance binder	to		
1105. Document preparation	to		

This is the back of the RESPA Good Faith Estimate and Settlement Statement. Pay particular attention and compare carefully the expenses being charged to you on the final settlement statement as opposed to the estimate given

1106. Notary fees	to	
1107. Attorney's fees	to	
(includes above items numbers:	)	
1108. Title insurance	to	
(includes above items numbers:	)	
1109. Lender's coverage	$	
1110. Owner's coverage	$	
1111.		
1112.		
1113.		
1200. Government Recording and Transfer Charges		
1201. Recording fees: Deed $	; Mortgage $	; Releases $
1202. City/county tax/stamps: Deed $	; Mortgage $	
1203. State tax/stamps: Deed $	; Mortgage $	
1204.		
1205.		
1300. Additional Settlement Charges		
1301. Survey to		
1302. Pest inspection to		
1303.		
1304.		
1305.		
1400. Total Settlement Charges (enter on lines 103, Section J and 502, Section K)		

Previous editions are obsolete   Page 2 of 2   form **HUD-1** (3/86) ref Handbook 4305.2

to you by the lender at loan application. There are frequent errors made here resulting in overcharges to the borrower. For more details, see discussion in the text.

use is designed to calculate interest on a declining balance method, with rigorously equal payments every month.

Now, at this point I have to ask you to think really hard — I'm going to get into math here. Don't panic! It's really easy math! I promise you can handle it with just ordinary brains.

OK, here goes. When you borrow money you make the first payment later, usually a month later. You certainly don't make the first payment on the day you borrow the money. And the interest is included in each payment, so it stands to reason that the interest is being collected at the end of each period. In other words, when we say "the April first payment" we mean the payment that is due on April 1, but which pays the interest for March. Similarly, the May payment will pay the interest for April, and so on.

Let's suppose your house closes on April 20. Your first payment will be due June 1, not May 1, because there must be a full month before the payment is due. And the June 1 payment will include interest for all of May. But notice that the lender is getting gypped here. You borrowed the money on April 20, and the lender is getting interest starting only on May 1.

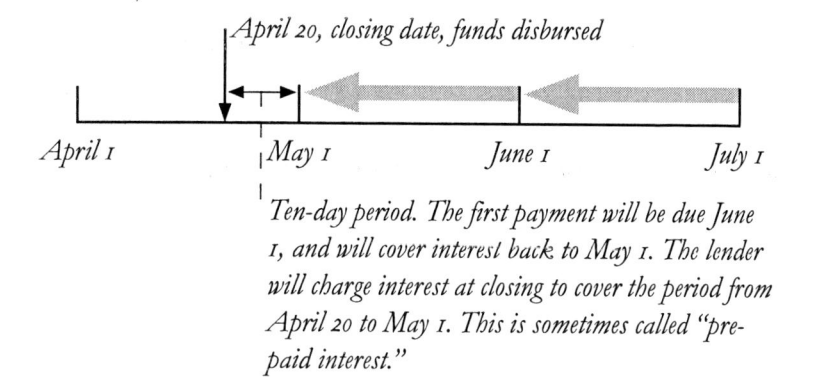

April 20, closing date, funds disbursed

April 1   May 1   June 1   July 1

Ten-day period. The first payment will be due June 1, and will cover interest back to May 1. The lender will charge interest at closing to cover the period from April 20 to May 1. This is sometimes called "prepaid interest."

No lender is going to let you get away with this. The lender wants interest for the last ten days of April. And the lender will instruct the closing agent to charge you for it at closing. On the form, this is on line 901.

So far, so good. The closing agent calculates interest all the time and can do this easily. The problem is that closing dates are invariably delayed. Every day that the closing gets closer to the first of the next month, you owe that much less "prepaid interest." And that is where errors happen. When the closing is delayed, it is very common for the closing agent to forget to recalculate how many days of prepaid interest you owe. I don't know about you, but I pay enough interest to banks without giving them interest they're not entitled to.

I've never had a closing agent miscalculate the dollar amount of interest once they had the right number of days. But I very frequently find the number of days is too many. So my advice is to check the dates on line 901 to make sure they start with the day you are really closing.

Line 902 is for the initial premium for the mortgage insurance. This protects the lender in the event of default. If your loan is 80% loan to value ratio or lower, there should be no mortgage insurance. Some lenders require that you pay the premium in advance for the first six months or a year. With some lenders there are other expenses involved in the private mortgage insurance. (For more discussion of this, see the chapter on loan programs — and check the private mortgage insurers listed in the Resources section at the back of this book.)

Once in a while I also find a closing agent will double-charge a borrower for the hazard insurance (line 903). "Hazard insurance" means your fire insurance policy on the new house. Lenders will not authorize release of the loan funds until they know the house is insured, so you will need to have coverage bound by closing date. However, occasionally a borrower will arrange this with his or her insurance agent outside of escrow, and will pay the agent directly. If the closing agent doesn't know the borrower did this, the borrower can end up getting charged for it again on the closing statement. The best practice is to go ahead and let the closing agent pay the insurance company directly. Most lenders prefer this anyway, and some require it. In other words, don't pay for the insurance yourself directly to the agent.

Section 1000 is for reserves for future expenses. In the northwest, that means your fire insurance premium and the county property tax bill. Do you remember back in the chapter on qualifying where we discussed the fact that your monthly payment includes the principal and interest, plus one-twelfth the annual fire insurance premium and one-twelfth the annual property tax bill? The lender takes the insurance and property tax portions of your monthly payment and puts it into a "reserve account" in your name. Some lenders call the reserve account an "escrow" or "impound" account. This is your money. The lender will use it to pay these expenses when they come due.

The problem is that the tax bill may come due too soon. In Oregon, property tax bills are due annually on November 15. In Washington they are due April 30. Let's suppose you're in Oregon and you close the sale of the house in the middle of the summer. By the time November 15 arrives you will have made only three or four payments. There will not be enough in your reserve account to pay the full tax bill. In anticipation of this problem, the lender will require the closing agent to collect from you enough toward the taxes so that, adding the amount from the payments that you will make by the tax due date, the reserve account will have enough to pay the tax bill.

Now, the problem is that lenders are a conservative lot. Furthermore, they tend to be a bit on the greedy side. They don't have to pay interest on the reserves, so they get the use of your money free. Therefore, the lender would like the reserve account to be as big as they can make it. In the past lenders abused this greatly, so much so that RESPA now restricts the amount they can require in the reserve account to the number of months actually needed, plus two. Nevertheless, lenders still try to pull a fast one from time to time. If you have any questions about how the reserves were calculated, ask the closing agent to go over it with you. Never be shy about asking these things. Closing agents are accustomed to it. Every closing agent I have ever known has told me they would rather take all the time necessary to explain things to the parties at closing, than have questions and complaints come up later.

The only items that should be charged to you in Section 1100 are one-half the closing fee (line 1101) and the lender's title insurance (line 1109). Unless, of course, you modified the standard earnest money form and agreed to pay expenses that are normally considered seller expenses. And if you're buying with a federal GI loan, you won't even be charged one-half the closing fee.

Over the years I have found that sellers and buyers are totally confused about title insurance, so let me take a moment and clarify things. There has to be some way for the sellers to prove to you (and to your lender) that they have good title. In the old days, the seller would provide the buyer with an abstract of title. Abstracts have not been used anywhere in the northwest for at least 50 years, having been replaced completely by title insurance.

In a purchase which is financed there will be two title insurance policies. One will insure the buyer — called the "owner's policy," because you will get it as soon as you become the new owner. The other insures the lender (called the "mortgagee's policy"). The terms of the lender's policy are different from the owner's policy. Your policy, for example, will insure that you have good title. The lender's policy will insure that their mortgage is a valid lien on your title. And the lender's policy is issued in the amount of the loan balance, with a clause stating that the coverage declines as the loan is paid off. Your policy, however, will be for the purchase price.

It is traditional for the seller to pay the premium for the buyer's (owner's) policy. But since it is your lender who is requiring the lender's policy, the lender's policy is considered a buyer expense. However, you are the lucky one in the deal. Title insurance companies charge less for the lender's policy than they do for the owner's policy, as long as it is issued at the same time as an owner's policy. So we make the seller pay the full premium for the owner's policy, and then the premium you pay for the lender's policy is only a portion of this in addition.

Title insurance premiums are based on the dollar amount of coverage. The premium for an owner's policy for a $125,000 house will vary a bit, but should run somewhere in the neighborhood of $600. The lender's policy, if issued at the same time, will cost about $150 extra. Title insurance coverage is forever, but the premium is a one-time charge at the time the policy is issued.

There is one occasion where a buyer may end up paying part of the premium for the owner's policy. The language of all the earnest money agreements in common use throughout the northwest call for the seller to pay the premium for a "standard form" owner's policy insuring the buyer's title. Normally, there is nothing wrong with a standard form policy. However, a standard form policy does not cover liens from contractors and other workers who claim they weren't paid for improvements they made to the property. If the property is not new construction and has not undergone renovation within the past few months, this is not a concern. But if there has been work done recently on the house, I always recommend to buyers that they consider paying a little extra to upgrade their coverage to an "extended coverage policy" which covers such liens. None of us likes paying insurance premiums, but they sure look like a bargain right after we have a loss.

Buyers and sellers also get confused about recording and the need for it (Section 1200). Although the amounts involved are usually very small, it wouldn't hurt to be aware of who normally pays for recording which documents, and why the expense exists in the first place.

Every county throughout the northwest (and in other states as well) has a county recording officer. The person with this duty may have other duties too, so the recording officer's title differs from one county to the next. The recording officer is responsible for keeping records of all documents that have been handed in for recording. In the old days (and still in a few small outlying counties) the recording officer would take each document and bind it into a book, giving it a page number in the process. Thus, from that day forward, everyone could refer to the document by the book number and page number. I remember walking into the office of the recording officer in Klickitat County, Washington once many years ago. The walls were lined with volumes filled with deeds, mortgages, contracts, and all manner of documents that people had handed in to be recorded. Every land transaction since the county was founded was in there.

Of course, imagine if the recorder for King County, Washington (Seattle) were to try to maintain physical books full of documents. They'd have to build a huge skyscraper to hold it all. So when the volume gets too large, we move to microfilm, microfiche, and other more compact storage media. The process is the same, however.

Recording a document protects the parties because it can't be lost. Even if you lose your copy of the deed to your house, for example, once it has been recorded there is a way to get a copy of it. It also provides certain other legal protections to the parties. Therefore, all the important documents in your closing must be recorded — specifically, the loan documents and your deed from the seller. If the sellers are paying off an old loan, there will be a document from their lender stating that it is paid in full and releasing the lien. This must be recorded too.

Recording fees vary a lot, but are never very much — usually no more than $20-30 or so per document. The buyer is expected to pay the charge for recording the buyer's loan documents, and usually also for recording the deed. The sellers are expected to pay the charge for recording the release of the lien from their old lender. I've never seen a closing agent get the amount of the fee wrong. But I have occasionally seen them charge the wrong party for a recording fee. Make sure you are being charged only for the deed and your own loan documents.

The real estate transfer tax is an expense only in Washington. The law does not stipulate which party must pay it, but it is common practice for the seller to pay the tax.

The only other expense that is normally charged to the buyer is the survey fee. Actually, this is not what you usually think of as a survey. Normally, a surveyor is hired to set out or locate the boundaries of the property. If you are buying an existing property, you'd surely think it was surveyed many years ago, wouldn't you?

The problem is not that the property boundaries cannot be located; it is that adjacent owners, or the sellers of the property themselves, may have built improvements over the years which encroach across the boundary. Encroachments are covered by the lender's title insurance policy. To protect themselves, title insurance companies require a certification by a surveyor that there are no encroachments before they will issue the lender's policy. Since the loan is what precipitated all this, the "survey fee" is considered normally a buyer expense.

It's not really a survey, though. What really happens is the surveyor drives by the property and fills out the certification as long as it appears there are no encroachments. If it were really a survey it would cost a lot more than the $50 or so that you will be charged for it. Once in a great while the surveyor actually finds an encroachment, in which case the whole transaction will be held up until it is resolved.

Of course, it is possible that you will be asked to pay for a real survey, but that would happen only if you are buying a parcel that has never been surveyed before. For example, suppose you are buying ten acres off the corner of the seller's land. Then someone has to set out the boundaries. Such a survey will cost hundreds of dollars. But if that happens you will have negotiated with the seller at the time of making the offer which of you will pay for it. And there will be lots of other expenses as well, since land divisions usually have to go through county planning and zoning review.

In my experience, at least one out of four closing statements contain an initial error, usually in favor of someone other than the buyer. The amount is usually small, but on occasion the mistake is significant. To protect my clients I always provide buyers with my own estimate of what the total cash requirement will be at closing, although most agents do not. Even if your agent does not, you can use the lender's good faith estimate as a guide. Compare the expense section carefully to the corresponding lines on the final closing statement and don't sign until everything is clear to you. Remember, the only stupid question is the one not asked.

Trust everybody, but cut the cards.
FINLEY PETER DUNNE

Appendix A

Seller Property Disclosure Forms

Both Oregon and Washington require sellers to give buyers of one- to four-family structures a disclosure regarding the condition of the property. Both states exempt transactions such as sales of brand new residences, and transactions that are not really sales, such as foreclosure transfers, inheritances, etc.

Oregon also exempts properties not to be occupied by the buyer or the buyer's family, and properties that have never been occupied by the seller. These exemptions are not available in Washington.

In Washington, unless exempt, the seller is required to deliver the disclosure statement to the buyer. The buyer has three days to cancel the transaction after receiving the form. Failure to do so means the buyer may back out of the transaction at any time right up to closing. If the buyer backs out the buyer is entitled to a full refund of everything the buyer paid up to that time. After closing, however, the buyer is no longer entitled to cancel the transaction or to any refunds.

In Oregon the provisions are the same, except that the seller may deliver a short "disclaimer form" instead of the disclosure form. The disclaimer form essentially says that the seller is not going to give the buyer the disclosure form and that the buyer takes the property as is. If the seller gives the buyer the disclosure form the buyer has five days to cancel the transaction. If the seller uses the disclaimer form instead, then the buyer has seven days to cancel. As in Washington, if the sellers decline to give the buyer either form, then the buyer may cancel at any time up to closing. Once the transaction closes there is no further right to cancel the transaction or to any refunds.

Buyers should not only always insist on the disclosure form, they should read it carefully as well. The sellers are liable to you for damages if they misrepresent or fail to disclose a material, latent defect in the property. But stating the defect on the disclosure form is adequate disclosure under the law. The fact that they did not also tell you to your face is irrelevant. You will be unable to claim damages as long as the disclosure is on the form. Therefore it is essential to go over the form carefully and ask questions about anything you do not understand.

Buyers in either state should be extremely careful buying property where the sellers do not give you a disclosure form. Refusing to do so is the same as saying they have something to hide. Assume the worst and hire a thorough inspection. Even an inspection may be inadequate, as there are items on the disclosure form that an inspection would not normally cover (condition of water rights, condition of the title, etc.).

The forms for Oregon and Washington as prescribed by each state's statutes are included on the following pages.

Oregon Seller Disclosure Form

Seller's Property Disclosure Statement
(Not a Warranty)
(105.465)

Instructions to the Seller

Please complete the following form. Do not leave any spaces blank unless the question clearly does not apply to the property. Please refer to the line number(s) of the question(s) when you provide your explanation(s). For your protection you must date and sign each page of this disclosure statement and each attachment.

Notice to the Buyer

THE FOLLOWING REPRESENTATIONS ARE MADE BY THE SELLER(S), CONCERNING THE CONDITION OF THE PROPERTY LOCATED AT _____ ("THE PROPERTY").

DISCLOSURES CONTAINED IN THIS FORM ARE PROVIDED BY THE SELLER ON THE BASIS OF SELLER'S ACTUAL KNOWLEDGE OF THE PROPERTY AT THE TIME OF DISCLOSURE. YOU HAVE FIVE BUSINESS DAYS FROM THE SELLER'S DELIVERY OF THIS SELLER'S DISCLOSURE STATEMENT TO REVOKE YOUR OFFER BY DELIVERING YOUR SEPARATE SIGNED WRITTEN STATEMENT OF REVOCATION TO THE SELLER, UNLESS YOU WAIVE THIS RIGHT AT OR PRIOR TO ENTERING INTO A SALE AGREEMENT.

FOR A MORE COMPREHENSIVE EXAMINATION OF THE SPECIFIC CONDITION OF THIS PROPERTY YOU ARE ADVISED TO OBTAIN AND PAY FOR THE SERVICES OF A QUALIFIED SPECIALIST TO INSPECT THE PROPERTY ON YOUR BEHALF, FOR EXAMPLE, ARCHITECTS, ENGINEERS, PLUMBERS, ELECTRICIANS, ROOFERS, BUILDING INSPECTORS, OR PEST AND DRY ROT INSPECTORS.

Seller _____ is/_____ is not occupying the property.

I. Seller's Representations:

The following are representations made by the seller and are not the representations of any financial institution that may have made or may make a loan pertaining to the property, or that may have or take a security interest in the property.

1. TITLE

Appendix A, Seller Property Disclosure Forms 191

☐ Yes ☐ No A. Do you have legal authority to sell the property?
☐ Yes ☐ No * B. To your knowledge, is title to the property subject to any of the following:
(1) First right of refusal
(2) Option
(3) Lease or rental agreement
(4) Other listing
(5) Life estate?
☐ Yes ☐ No * C. Are you aware of any encroachments, boundary agreements, boundary disputes or recent boundary changes?
☐ Yes ☐ No * D. Are you aware of any rights of way, easements or licenses (access limitations) that may affect your interest in the property?
☐ Yes ☐ No * E. Are you aware of any written agreements for joint maintenance of an easement or right of way?
☐ Yes ☐ No F. Are you aware of any governmental study, survey or notices that would affect the property?
☐ Yes ☐ No G. Are you aware of any pending or existing assessments against the property?
☐ Yes ☐ No H. Are you aware of any zoning violations or nonconforming uses?
☐ Yes ☐ No * I. Are you aware of a boundary survey for the property?
☐ Yes ☐ No * J. Are you aware of any covenants, conditions or restrictions which affect the property?

2. WATER

A. Household Water
(1) The source of the water is:
☐ Public ☐ Community
☐ Private ☐ Shared

(2) Water source information:
☐ Yes ☐ No * a. Are you aware of any written agreements for shared water source?
☐ Yes ☐ No * b. To your knowledge, is there an easement (recorded or unrecorded) for access to and/or maintenance of the water source?
☐ Yes ☐ No c. Are any known problems or repairs needed?
☐ Yes ☐ No (3) Are you aware of any water treatment systems for the property?
☐ Leased ☐ Owned

B. Irrigation
☐ Yes ☐ No (1) Are you aware of any water rights for the property?
☐ Yes ☐ No * (2) If there exist any, to your knowledge, have the water water rights been used during the last five-year period?
☐ Yes ☐ No * (3) If so, is the certificate available?

C. Outdoor Sprinkler system
☐ Yes ☐ No (1) To your knowledge, is there an outdoor sprinkler system for the property?
☐ Yes ☐ No (2) To your knowledge, has a back flow valve been installed?
☐ Yes ☐ No (3) To your knowledge, is the outdoor sprinkler system operable?

3. SEWAGE
☐ Yes ☐ No A. To your knowledge, is the property connected to a sanitary sewer?
☐ Yes ☐ No B. Are you aware of any sanitary sewer proposed for the property?
☐ Yes ☐ No C. To your knowledge, is the property connected to a septic system or cesspool?
☐ Yes ☐ No D. Are you aware of any problems or repairs needed?
☐ Yes ☐ No E. To your knowledge, does your sewage system require on-site pumping to another level?

4. INSULATION

A. To your knowledge, is there insulation in the:
☐ Yes ☐ No (1) Ceiling?
☐ Yes ☐ No (2) Exterior walls?
☐ Yes ☐ No (3) Floors?
☐ Yes ☐ No B. To your knowledge, are there any defective insulated windows?

5. STRUCTURAL
☐ Yes ☐ No * A. To your knowledge, has the roof leaked?
☐ Yes ☐ No If yes, has it been repaired?
☐ Yes ☐ No B. Additions/conversions/remodeling?
☐ Yes ☐ No * If yes, are you aware of whether a building permit was obtained?
☐ Yes ☐ No Was final inspection obtained?
☐ Yes ☐ No C. To your knowledge, are there smoke alarms?
☐ Yes ☐ No If there are, which are electrical (hard-wired)?
☐ Yes ☐ No D. To your knowledge, is there a woodstove? Make _____
☐ Yes ☐ No Was it installed with a permit?
☐ Yes ☐ No * E. Are you aware of whether a pest or dry rot, structural or "whole house" inspection has been done?
☐ Yes ☐ No * F. Are you aware of any moisture problems in the structure (especially in the basement)? If yes, explain frequency and extent of problem on attached sheet
☐ Yes ☐ No G. Are you aware of a sump pump on the property?

6. SYSTEMS AND FIXTURES
If the following systems or fixtures are included in the purchase price, are they, to your knowledge, in good working order on the date this form is signed?

❑ Yes ❑ No A. Electrical system, including wiring, switches, outlets and service
❑ Yes ❑ No B. Plumbing system, including pipes, faucets, fixtures and toilets
❑ Yes ❑ No C. Hot water tank
❑ Yes ❑ No D. Garbage disposal
❑ Yes ❑ No E. Built-in range and oven
❑ Yes ❑ No F. Built-in dishwasher
❑ Yes ❑ No G. Sump pump
❑ Yes ❑ No H. Heating and cooling systems
❑ Yes ❑ No I. Security system ❑ Owned ❑ Leased

7. COMMON INTEREST
❑ Yes ❑ No A. Home Owners' Association?
Name of Association _____ Address _____ Contact Person _____
Phone Number _____
❑ Yes ❑ No B. Regular periodic assessments: $ _____ per ❑ Month ❑ Year ❑ Other _____
❑ Yes ❑ No C. Are you aware of any pending special assessments?
❑ Yes ❑ No D. Are you aware of any shared "common areas" or any joint maintenance agreements (facilities such as walls, fences, pools, tennis courts, walkways or other areas co-owned in undivided interest with others)?

8. GENERAL
❑ Yes ❑ No A. Are you aware of any settling, soil, standing water or drainage problems on the property or in the immediate area?

☐ Yes ☐ No B. To your knowledge, does the property contain fill?
☐ Yes ☐ No C. Are you aware of any material damage to the property or any of the structure from fire, wind, floods, beach movements, earthquake, expansive soils or landslides?
☐ Yes ☐ No D. To your knowledge, is the property in a designated flood plain?
☐ Yes ☐ No E. To your knowledge, is the property in a designated slide zone?
☐ Yes ☐ No F. Are you aware of any substances, materials or products that may be an environmental hazard such as, but not limited to, asbestos, formaldehyde, radon gas, lead based paint, fuel or chemical storage tanks, and contaminated soil or water on the subject property?
☐ Yes ☐ No G. Are you aware of any tanks or underground storage tanks (e.g, septic, chemical, fuel, etc.) on the property?
☐ Yes ☐ No H. To your knowledge, has the property ever been used as an illegal drug manufacturing site?
9. FULL DISCLOSURE BY SELLERS
A. Other conditions or defects
☐ Yes ☐ No Are you aware of any other material defects affecting this property or its value that a prospective buyer should know about?
B. Verification

The foregoing answers and attached explanations (if any) are complete and correct to the best of my/our knowledge and I/we have received a copy hereof. I/we authorize all of my/our agents to deliver a copy of this disclosure statement to other real estate licensees and all prospective buyers of the property.

DATE _____

SELLER _____ SELLER _____

II. Buyer's Acknowledgment

A. As buyer(s), I/we acknowledge the duty to pay diligent attention to any material defects which are known to me/us or can be known by me/us by utilizing diligent attention and observation.

B. Each buyer acknowledges and understands that the disclosures set forth in this statement and in any amendments to this statement are made only by the seller and are not the representations of any financial institution that may have made or may make a loan pertaining to the property, or that may have or take a security interest in the property and no such financial institution shall be bound by or have any liability with respect to any representation, misrepresentation, omission, error or inaccuracy contained in another party's disclosure statement required by this section or any amendment to the disclosure statement.

C. Buyer (which term includes all persons signing the "buyer's acceptance" portion of this disclosure statement below) hereby acknowledges receipt of a copy of this disclosure statement (including attachments, if any) bearing seller's signature. DISCLOSURES CONTAINED IN THIS FORM ARE PROVIDED BY THE SELLER ON THE BASIS OF SELLER'S ACTUAL KNOWLEDGE OF THE PROPERTY AT THE TIME OF DISCLOSURE. YOU, THE BUYER, HAVE FIVE BUSINESS DAYS FROM THE SELLER'S DELIVERY OF THIS SELLER'S DISCLOSURE STATEMENT TO REVOKE YOUR OFFER BY DELIVERING YOUR SEPARATE SIGNED WRITTEN STATEMENT OF REVOCATION TO THE SELLER UNLESS YOU WAIVE THIS RIGHT AT OR PRIOR TO ENTERING INTO A SALE AGREEMENT.

Buyer hereby acknowledges receipt of a copy of this seller's disclosure statement.

Date_____

Buyer_____ Buyer_____

Agent to sign and date:

_____ Real Estate Licensee
_____ Real Estate Organization

*If yes, attach a copy or explain on attached sheet

Washington Seller Disclosure Form

Instructions to the Seller

Please complete the following form. Do not leave any spaces blank. If the question clearly does not apply to the property write "NA". If the answer is "YES" to any * items, please explain on attached sheets. Please refer to the line number(s) of the question(s) when you provide your explanation(s). For your protection you must date and sign each page of this disclosure statement and each attachment. Delivery of the disclosure statement must occur not later than five business days, unless otherwise agreed, after mutual acceptance of a written contract to purchase between a buyer and a seller.

Notice to the Buyer

The following disclosures are made by the seller(s), concerning the condition of the property located at _____

("the property"), or as legally described on attached exhibit A.

Disclosures contained in this form are provided by the seller on the basis of seller's actual knowledge of the property at the time this disclosure form is completed by the seller. You have three business days, unless otherwise agreed, from the seller's delivery of this seller's disclosure statement to rescind your agreement by delivering your separate signed written statement of rescission to the seller, unless you waive this right at or prior to entering into a sale agreement. The following are disclosures made by the seller and are not the representations of any real estate licensee or other party. This information is for disclosure only and is not intended to be a part of any written agreement between the buyer and the seller.

For a more comprehensive examination of the specific condition of this property you are advised to obtain

AND PAY FOR THE SERVICES OF A QUALIFIED SPECIALIST TO INSPECT THE PROPERTY ON YOUR BEHALF, FOR EXAMPLE, ARCHITECTS, ENGINEERS, LAND SURVEYORS, PLUMBERS, ELECTRICIANS, ROOFERS, BUILDING INSPECTORS, OR PEST AND DRY ROT INSPECTORS. THE PROSPECTIVE BUYER AND THE OWNER MAY WISH TO OBTAIN PROFESSIONAL ADVICE OR INSPECTIONS OF THE PROPERTY AND TO PROVIDE FOR APPROPRIATE PROVISIONS IN A CONTRACT BETWEEN THEM WITH RESPECT TO ANY ADVICE, INSPECTION, DEFECTS OR WARRANTIES.

Seller ❏ is/ ❏ is not occupying the property.

I. SELLER'S DISCLOSURES:

*If "Yes" attach a copy or explain. If necessary use an attached sheet.

1. TITLE

❏ Yes ❏ No ❏ Don't know A. Do you have legal authority to sell the property?
❏ Yes ❏ No ❏ Don't know *B. Is title to the property subject to any of the following? (1) First right of refusal (2) Option (3) Lease or rental agreement (4) Life estate?
❏ Yes ❏ No ❏ Don't know *C. Are there any encroachments, boundary agreements, or boundary disputes?
❏ Yes ❏ No ❏ Don't know *D. Are there any rights of way, easements, or access limitations that may affect the owner's use of the property?
❏ Yes ❏ No ❏ Don't know *E. Are there any written agreements for joint maintenance of an easement or right of way?
❏ Yes ❏ No ❏ Don't know *F. Is there any study, survey project, or notice that would adversely affect the property?
❏ Yes ❏ No ❏ Don't know *G. Are there any pending or existing assessments against the property?
❏ Yes ❏ No ❏ Don't know *H. Are there any zoning violations, nonconforming uses, or any unusual restrictions on the subject property that would affect future construction or remodeling?

☐ Yes ☐ No ☐ Don't know *I. Is there a boundary survey for the property?
☐ Yes ☐ No ☐ Don't know *J. Are there any covenants, conditions, or restrictions which affect the property?

2. WATER A. Household Water (i) The source of the water is
☐ Public ☐ Community
☐ Private ☐ Shared

(2) Water source information:
☐ Yes ☐ No ☐ Don't know *a. Are there any written agreements for shared water source?
☐ Yes ☐ No ☐ Don't know *b. Is there an easement (recorded or unrecorded) for access to and/or maintenance of the water source?
☐ Yes ☐ No ☐ Don't know *c. Are any known problems or repairs needed?
☐ Yes ☐ No ☐ Don't know *d. Does the source provide an adequate year round supply of potable water?
☐ Yes ☐ No ☐ Don't know *(3) Are there any water treatment systems for the property? ☐ Leased ☐ Owned

B. Irrigation
☐ Yes ☐ No ☐ Don't know (1) Are there any water rights for the property?
☐ Yes ☐ No ☐ Don't know *(2) If they exist, to your knowledge, have the water rights been used during the last five-year period?
☐ Yes ☐ No ☐ Don't know *(3) If so, is the certificate available?

C. Outdoor Sprinkler System
☐ Yes ☐ No ☐ Don't know (1) Is there an outdoor sprinkler system for the property?
☐ Yes ☐ No ☐ Don't know *(2) Are there any defects in the outdoor sprinkler system?

3. SEWER/SEPTIC SYSTEM A. The property is served by:
☐ Public sewer main, ☐ Septic tank system ☐ Other disposal system (describe) _____

Appendix A, Seller Property Disclosure Forms 201

☐ Yes ☐ No ☐ Don't know B. If the property is served by a public or community sewer main, is the house connected to the main? C. Is the property currently subject to a sewer capacity charge?
D. If the property is connected to a septic system:
☐ Yes ☐ No ☐ Don't know (1) Was a permit issued for its construction, and was it approved by the city or county following its construction? (2) When was it last pumped: _____, 20____
☐ Yes ☐ No ☐ Don't know *(3) Are there any defects in the operation of the septic system?
☐ Don't know (4) When was it last inspected? _____, 20____ By Whom: _____
☐ Don't know (5) How many bedrooms was the system approved for? _____ bedrooms
☐ Yes ☐ No ☐ Don't know *E. Do all plumbing fixtures, including laundry drain, go to the septic/sewer system? If no, explain: _____
☐ Yes ☐ No ☐ Don't know *F. Are you aware of any changes or repairs to the septic system?
☐ Yes ☐ No ☐ Don't know G. Is the septic tank system, including the drainfield, located entirely within the boundaries of the property?

4. STRUCTURAL

☐ Yes ☐ No ☐ Don't know *A. Has the roof leaked?
☐ Yes ☐ No ☐ Don't know *If yes, has it been repaired?
☐ Yes ☐ No ☐ Don't know *B. Have there been any conversions, additions, or remodeling?
☐ Yes ☐ No ☐ Don't know *1. If yes, were all building permits obtained?
☐ Yes ☐ No ☐ Don't know *2. If yes, were all final inspections obtained?
☐ Yes ☐ No ☐ Don't know C. Do you know the age of the house? If yes, year of original construction: _____
☐ Yes ☐ No ☐ Don't know *D. Do you know of any settling, slippage, or sliding of either the house or other structures/improvements located on the property? If yes, explain: _____

☐ Yes ☐ No ☐ Don't know *E. Do you know of any defects with the following: (Please check applicable items) ☐ Foundations ☐ Decks ☐ Exterior Walls ☐ Chimneys ☐ Interior Walls ☐ Fire Alarm ☐ Doors ☐ Windows ☐ Patio ☐ Ceilings ☐ Slab Floors ☐ Driveways ☐ Pools ☐ Hot Tub ☐ Sauna ☐ Sidewalks ☐ Outbuildings ☐ Fireplaces ☐ Garage Floors ☐ Walkways ☐ Other ☐ Wood Stoves

☐ Yes ☐ No ☐ Don't know *F. Was a pest or dry rot, structural or "whole house" inspection done? When and by whom was the inspection completed? _____

☐ Yes ☐ No ☐ Don't know *G. Since assuming ownership, has your property had a problem with wood destroying organisms and/or have there been any problems with pest control, infestations, or vermin?

5. SYSTEMS AND FIXTURES If the following systems or fixtures are included with the transfer, do they have any existing defects:

☐ Yes ☐ No ☐ Don't know *A. Electrical system, including wiring, switches, outlets, and service
☐ Yes ☐ No ☐ Don't know *B. Plumbing system, including pipes, faucets, fixtures, and toilets
☐ Yes ☐ No ☐ Don't know *C. Hot water tank
☐ Yes ☐ No ☐ Don't know *D. Garbage disposal
☐ Yes ☐ No ☐ Don't know *E. Appliances
☐ Yes ☐ No ☐ Don't know *F. Sump pump
☐ Yes ☐ No ☐ Don't know *G. Heating and cooling systems
☐ Yes ☐ No ☐ Don't know *H. Security system
☐ Owned ☐ Leased I. Other _____

6. COMMON INTEREST

☐ Yes ☐ No ☐ Don't know A. Is there a Home Owners' Association? Name of Association _____

❏ Yes ❏ No ❏ Don't know B. Are there regular periodic assessments: $_____ per ❏ Month ❏ Year
❏ Other _____
❏ Yes ❏ No ❏ Don't know *C. Are there any pending special assessments?
❏ Yes ❏ No ❏ Don't know *D. Are there any shared "common areas" or any joint maintenance agreements (facilities such as walls, fences, landscaping, pools, tennis courts, walkways, or other areas co-owned in undivided interest with others)?

7. GENERAL
❏ Yes ❏ No ❏ Don't know *A. Is there any settling, soil, standing water, or drainage problems on the property?
❏ Yes ❏ No ❏ Don't know *B. Does the property contain fill material?
❏ Yes ❏ No ❏ Don't know *C. Is there any material damage to the property or any of the structure from fire, wind, floods, beach movements, earthquake, expansive soils, or landslides?
❏ Yes ❏ No ❏ Don't know D. Is the property in a designated flood plain?
❏ Yes ❏ No ❏ Don't know *E. Are there any substances, materials, or products that may be an environmental hazard such as, but not limited to, asbestos, formaldehyde, radon gas, lead-based paint, fuel or chemical storage tanks, and contaminated soil or water on the subject property?
❏ Yes ❏ No ❏ Don't know *F. Are there any tanks or underground storage tanks (e.g., chemical, fuel, etc.) on the property?
❏ Yes ❏ No ❏ Don't know *G. Has the property ever been used as an illegal drug manufacturing site?

8. FULL DISCLOSURE BY SELLERS
A. Other conditions or defects:
❏ Yes ❏ No ❏ Don't know *Are there any other material defects affecting this property or its value that a prospective buyer should know about? B. Verification: The foregoing answers and attached explanations (if any) are complete and correct to the best of my/our knowledge and I/we have received a copy hereof. I/we authorize all of

my/our real estate licensees, if any, to deliver a copy of this disclosure statement to other real estate licensees and all prospective buyers of the property.

DATE _____
SELLER _____
SELLER _____

II. BUYER'S ACKNOWLEDGMENT A. As buyer(s), I/we acknowledge the duty to pay diligent attention to any material defects which are known to me/us or can be known to me/us by utilizing diligent attention and observation. B. Each buyer acknowledges and understands that the disclosures set forth in this statement and in any amendments to this statement are made only by the seller. C. Buyer (which term includes all persons signing the "buyer's acceptance" portion of this disclosure statement below) hereby acknowledges receipt of a copy of this disclosure statement (including attachments, if any) bearing seller's signature.

DISCLOSURES CONTAINED IN THIS FORM ARE PROVIDED BY THE SELLER ON THE BASIS OF SELLER'S ACTUAL KNOWLEDGE OF THE PROPERTY AT THE TIME OF DISCLOSURE. YOU, THE BUYER, HAVE THREE BUSINESS DAYS, UNLESS OTHERWISE AGREED, FROM THE SELLER'S DELIVERY OF THIS SELLER'S DISCLOSURE STATEMENT TO RESCIND YOUR AGREEMENT BY DELIVERING YOUR SEPARATE SIGNED WRITTEN STATEMENT OF RESCISSION TO THE SELLER UNLESS YOU WAIVE THIS RIGHT OF RESCISSION. BUYER HEREBY ACKNOWLEDGES RECEIPT OF A COPY OF THIS REAL PROPERTY TRANSFER DISCLOSURE STATEMENT AND ACKNOWLEDGES THAT THE DISCLOSURES MADE HEREIN ARE THOSE OF THE SELLER ONLY, AND NOT OF ANY REAL ESTATE LICENSEE OR OTHER PARTY.

DATE _____
BUYER _____
BUYER _____

Appendix B

Amortization Chart

Amortization Chart

This chart shows the monthly payment necessary to amortize a loan of $1,000 at varying interest rates (top row) for one to thirty years (left column). To find the payment for loans greater than $1,000, multiply the appropriate factor below by the number of thousands in the loan. For example, a loan of $258,000 at 7% interest for 30 years would use the factor $6.65. This is the amount for a $1,000 loan, so for a loan of $258,000, multiply the factor by 258. The total payment is therefore $1,715.70 ($6.65 × 258 = $1,715.70).

Years	6%	7%	8%	9%	10%	11%	12%
1	86.06	86.53	86.99	87.45	87.92	88.38	88.49
2	44.32	44.77	45.23	45.68	46.15	46.61	47.07
3	30.42	30.88	31.34	31.80	32.27	32.74	33.21
4	23.49	23.95	24.41	24.89	25.36	25.85	26.33
5	19.33	19.80	20.28	20.76	21.25	21.74	22.24
6	16.57	17.05	17.53	18.03	18.53	19.03	19.55
7	14.61	15.09	15.59	16.09	16.60	17.12	17.65
8	13.14	13.63	14.14	14.65	15.17	15.71	16.25
9	12.01	12.51	13.01	13.54	14.08	14.63	15.18
10	11.10	11.61	12.13	12.67	13.22	13.78	14.35
11	10.37	10.88	11.42	11.96	12.52	13.09	13.68
12	9.76	10.28	10.82	11.38	11.95	12.54	13.13
13	9.25	9.78	10.33	10.90	11.48	12.08	12.69
14	8.81	9.35	9.91	10.49	11.08	11.69	12.31
15	8.44	8.99	9.55	10.14	10.75	11.37	12.00
16	8.11	8.67	9.25	9.85	10.46	11.09	11.74
17	7.83	8.40	8.98	9.59	10.21	10.85	11.51
18	7.58	8.16	8.75	9.36	10.00	10.65	11.32

Appendix B, Amortization Chart

19	7.36	7.94	8.55	9.17	9.81	10.47	11.15
20	7.16	7.75	8.36	9.00	9.65	10.32	11.01
21	6.99	7.58	8.20	8.85	9.51	10.19	10.87
22	6.83	7.43	8.06	8.71	9.34	10.07	10.78
23	6.69	7.30	7.93	8.59	9.27	9.97	10.69
24	6.56	7.18	7.82	8.49	9.17	9.88	10.60
25	6.44	7.07	7.72	8.39	9.09	9.80	10.53
26	6.34	6.97	7.63	8.31	9.01	9.73	10.47
27	6.24	6.88	7.54	8.23	8.94	9.67	10.41
28	6.15	6.80	7.47	8.16	8.88	9.61	10.37
29	6.07	6.72	7.40	8.10	8.82	9.57	10.32
30	6.00	6.65	7.34	8.05	8.78	9.52	10.29

In times past real estate agents carried around small booklets of loan amortization tables, similar to the chart above, but broken down by quarters of a percent. Today, agents simply use an inexpensive financial calculator. For beginners, the Texas Instruments BA-35 is one of the most popular. The keystrokes to compute the monthly payment necessary for a $258,000 loan at 7% for 30 years on the BA-35 are —

258,000 **PV**

7 **2nd** **%i** (on some versions you must hit the **%i** key twice)

30 **2nd** **N** (on some versions you must hit the **N** key twice)

CPT **PMT**

Display 1,716.48

Note that the answer from the calculator is a few cents off from the results by using the chart. The reason is because the figures in the chart are rounded to the nearest cent, whereas the calculator holds the decimal to many places of accuracy. The factor used above for a 7% loan of 30 years is given as $6.65 in the chart, but the calculator uses the whole decimal — $6.653024953.

The nice thing about the financial calculator is that it allows quick what-if scenarios. If you want to know what the payment would be if the interest rate were 8% instead of 7%, all you have to do is enter the new percentage rate, then hit **CPT** **PMT** and the calculator will recalculate the payment. The calculator remembers what was entered in the **%i** and **N** registers.

Resources

The following are organizations and other resources of help to homebuyers. They are organized as follows:
- Affordable housing
- Credit reporting agencies and credit repair
- Home inspectors
- Licensing agencies and real estate laws
- Locating an agent
- Locating property
- Mortgage agencies (state, federal and private)
- Mortgage insurance companies
- Publications
- Research and statistics on housing

Where appropriate web site and e-mail addresses are included.

Affordable housing
- HomeSight, 3405 S. Alaska, Seattle, Washington 98118, 206-723-4153, 206-723-7137. HomeSight is a non-profit community development corporation that promotes the revitalization of Seattle's Central and Southeast neighborhoods through affordable home ownership strategies.
- Portland Housing Center, 1605 N.E. 45th Avenue, Portland, Oregon 97213, 503-282-7744. The Portland Housing Center is funded by local lenders and provides information for first-time homebuyers, low-income housing programs, and general home ownership issues.
- Spokane Neighborhood Action Programs (SNAP), 2116

E. First, Spokane, Washington 99202-3174, 509-456-7111, 509-534-5874. Programs include energy assistance, weatherization, emergency and minor home repairs, home rehabilitation, comprehensive housing counseling, housing development, and home ownership opportunities.

- Threshold Housing, 1100 Second Avenue, Suite 101, Seattle, Washington 98101, 206-585-8020, 206-585-8002. A nonprofit housing developer of demonstration projects. Typically targeted at first-time homebuyers, under 80% of median income. Financing assistance available for purchasers.
- Vancouver Housing Center, 5212 N.E. St. Johns Road, Vancouver, Washington 98661, 360-690-496. The Vancouver Housing Center is a nonprofit organization which does prepurchase counseling for first-time homebuyers and referrals to other resources.

Credit reporting agencies and credit repair

- Equifax, Post Office Box 740256, Atlanta, Georgia 30374-0256, 800-997-2493, web site http://www.consumer.equifax.com. To order a copy of your credit report by mail write to Equifax Consumer Services, Post Office Box 10596, Atlanta, Georgia 30348-5496. The cost of a credit report is $8.00.
- Experian (former name TRW), National Consumer Assistance Center, Post Office Box 9595, Allen, Texas 75013-0036, 888-397-3742, web site http:/www.experian.com. You may order a copy of your credit report for $8.50.
- Trans Union, Post Office Box 2000, Chester, Pennsylvania 19022, 800-916-8800 (to speak to a customer service representative) or 800-888-4213 to order a copy of your credit report for $8.00.
- Federal Trade Commission, Consumer Resource Center 420, Washington, D.C. 20580, 877-382-4357, web site http://www.ftc.gov/ftc/consumer.htm. The Federal Trade Commission enforces federal laws relating to credit repair agencies and offers consumer information to assist borrowers in repairing their credit.

Home inspectors

- American Society of Home Inspectors (ASHI), 932 Lee Street, Suite 101, DesPlaines, Illinois 60016, 800-743-2744. A nonprofit organization of home inspectors who have agreed to a code of ethics. Can provide names and phone numbers of members in Oregon and Washington. Web site http://www.ashi.com, which contains a search engine to find a local member.
- HouseMaster of America, 421 West Union Avenue, Bound Brook, New Jersey 08805, 800-526-3939. An organization of independently owned franchise home inspectors throughout the country, with numerous offices throughout Oregon and Washington. Web site http://www.housemaster.com, which contains a search engine to find a local office.

Licensing agencies and real estate laws

- Oregon Real Estate Agency, 1177 Center Street N.E., Salem, Oregon 97310-2505. To locate an agent by name or for other administrative questions call 503-378-4170. Complaints and general questions from the public are answered on a call-back basis at 503-378-8414. Note that the Real Estate Agency cannot answer legal questions or give opinions about a specific property. Their sole purpose is to ensure that licensees obey the licensing laws. Web site at http://bbs.chemek.cc.or.us/public/orea/orea.html.
- Oregon Revised Statutes (ORS). If you have any questions regarding real estate statutes in general, or real estate licensing laws, the entire text of Oregon Revised Statutes is online at http://landru.leg.state.or.us/ors/. You can also find copies at most public libraries. Statutory law is subject to interpretation by the courts and should be acted on only with advice from an attorney.
- Washington Real Estate Commission (Department of Licensing), Post Office Box 9015, Olympia, Washington 98507-9015. For general questions, to locate an agent by name, or to register a complaint about an agent call 360-586-4602. The Washington Real Estate Commission cannot give legal advice or answer specific questions about a property. E-mail to RealEstate@dol.wa.gov. Web site http://www.wa.gov/dol/bpd/refront.htm.
- Revised Code of Washington (RCW). The entire text

of the Revised Code of Washington is available online at http://www.leg.wa.gov/wsladm//rcw.htm, or you can search at http://search.leg.wa.gov/pub/textsearch/default.asp?. You can also find copies at most public libraries. Statutory law is subject to interpretation by the courts and should be acted on only with advice from an attorney.

Locating an agent

- Real Estate Buyers Agent Council of the National Association of Realtors® (REBAC), 430 N. Michigan Avenue, Chicago, Illinois 60611, 800-648-6224, e-mail rebac@realtors.org, web site http://www.rebac.net. Has many services for homebuyers, including facilities for referral to local agents who work as buyers' agents. Members can qualify to be designated as an ABR (Accredited Buyer Representative) or ABRM (Accredited Buyer Representative Manager) if they meet education and experience requirements. A subsidiary organization of the National Association of Realtors® (NAR). Members must also be members of NAR. Members are not necessarily exclusive buyers agents (may take listings as well).

- National Association of Exclusive Buyer Agents (NAEBA), 7652 Gartner Road, Suite 500, Evergreen, Colorado 80439-5204, 800-986-2322, e-mail to info@naeba.org, web site http://www.naeba.org. Offers many services to homebuyers including a listing of their members, all of whom act as exclusive buyers' agents (never take listings). Their web site includes a search engine to locate members in your area. Not affiliated with the National Association of Realtors® (NAR), although many of their members are also members of NAR.

Locating property

- CyberHomes, web-based property locator with search engine for Eugene, Portland, Bellingham, Seattle, Vancouver, Olympia, Yakima, and Stevens, Ferry and Pend Oreille counties. Web site http://www.cyberhomes.com. Web site also has other links of interest to homebuyers.

- National Association of Realtors® (NAR), 430 N. Michigan Avenue, Chicago, Illinois 60611. Web-based search engine covering 1.3 million homes listed by members nationwide. Web site http:// www.realtor.com.

Mortgage agencies

• Fannie Mae, Western Regional Office, 135 North Los Robles Avenue, Suite 300, Pasadena, California 91101-1707, 800-732-6643 (Consumer Resource Center), web site http://www.fanniemae.com. Fannie Mae is an investor-owned secondary lender, that is, it purchases loans originated by local lenders. Old name: Federal National Mortgage Association. Its stock is traded on the New York Stock Exchange.

• Federal Reserve Board, 20th Street and Constitution Avenue, N.W., Washington, D.C. 20551, web site http://www.bog.frb.fed.us. The Federal Reserve Board enforces the federal Truth in Lending Act and Federal Reserve Regulation z, both of which require lenders to disclose loan information such as the annual percentage rate (APR), Total Finance Charge, and other matters.

• Freddie Mac, 8200 Jones Branch Drive, Mclean, Virginia 22102-3110, 703-903-2000; Western Region Office, 21700 Oxnard Street, Suite 1900, Woodland Hills, California 91367-3621, 818-710-3000, web site http://www.freddiemac.com. Freddie Mac is an investor-owned secondary lender, that is, it purchases loans originated by local lenders. Original name: Federal National Mortgage Corporation. Its stock is traded on the New York Stock Exchange.

• Government National Mortgage Association (commonly called "Ginnie Mae"), 451 Seventh Street S.W., Washington, D.C. 20410-9000. Ginnie Mae is a government-owned purchaser of federally insured and guaranteed loans as a secondary lender. It normally has no direct contact with consumers.

• Oregon Department of Housing and Community Services, 1600 State Street, Salem, Oregon 97301-2426, 503-986-2000, web site http://www.hcs.state.or.us/geninfo/index.html. The Department of Housing and Community Services offers below-market rate mortgage loans from the proceeds of the sale of tax-exempt bonds. The bonds are sold to investors and the Department uses the money to purchase loans, which are made by lending institutions. Certain borrowers may also qualify to borrow a portion of their down payment.

• Oregon Department of Veterans Affairs, 700 Summer Street N.E., Salem, Oregon 97310, 503-373-2000 in Salem or 800-828-8801 from the rest of the state, web site http://www.odva.state.or.us. The Department makes direct loans to eligible veterans and surviving spouses at very attractive interest rates, although few veterans currently qualify. For eligibility information call 888-ORE-VETS.

• U.S. Department of Housing & Urban Development (HUD). A federal cabinet agency dealing with housing and community development programs. The Office of Housing administers Federal Housing Administration (FHA) single family and multi-family mortgage insurance programs, which enable home buyers to obtain home loans on favorable terms. General home ownership information is available toll-free at 888-827-5605, information about 1-4 family home loans, call 800-225-5342; to see if there are any HUD-acquired properties available for sale in your area, call 800-767-4483; for housing discrimination (Fair Housing Act) issues, call 800-669-9777; main web site http://www.hud.gov. HUD also administers the Real Estate Settlement Procedures Act, which has a separate web site at http://www.hud.gov/fha/res/respa_htm.html.

Washington State Office, 909 First Avenue, Suite 190, Seattle, Washington 98104-1000, 206-220-5200, 206-220-5206.

Oregon State Office, 400 S.W. Sixth Avenue, Suite 700, Portland, Oregon 97204-1632, 503-326-2561.

• U.S. Department of Agriculture, Rural Development, Rural Housing Service, Stop 0780, 1400 Independence Avenue S.W., Washington, D.C. 20250-0780, 202-720-1477, http://www.rurdev.usda.gov. In Oregon there are local offices in Eugene, Medford, Ontario, Pendleton, Redmond, Roseburg, Salem, St. Helens. Housing issues are handled at the Salem office, 503-399-5799. In Washington all information is handled at the Olympia office, 360-704-7707.

• U.S. Department of Veterans Affairs has two offices in the northwest. Both use the same toll-free number for information, 800-827-1000. There is also a regional loan processing center in

Denver (toll-free 888-349-7541) where you can sometimes get information on their loan programs more quickly. The national web site is http://homeloans.va.gov. Local office locations are —
Seattle Regional Office, 915 Second Avenue, Jackson Building, Seattle, Washington 98174-1001 http://www.seattleva.com.
Portland Regional Office, Edith Green Federal Office Building, 1220 S.W. Third Avenue, Portland, Oregon 97204, web site http://www.pmlgyport.com.

• Washington State Housing Finance Commission, 1000 Second Avenue, Suite 2700, Seattle, Washington 98104-1046, 206-464-7139 in the Seattle area, or 800-767-4663 in the rest of the state, web site http://www.washfc.org. The Commission has funds from the sale of tax-exempt bonds at low interest rates to purchase below-market rate loans from lenders participating in their programs. Certain borrowers may also qualify to borrow a portion of their down payment.

Mortgage insurance agencies

• Amerin Guaranty Corp, 200 E. Randolph Drive, 49th Floor, Chicago, Illinois 60601, 800-257-7653.

• Commonwealth Mortgage Assurance Company, 1601 Market Street, Philadelphia Pennsylvania, 19103-2107, 800-523-1988.

• GE Capital Mortgage Insurance Group, 6601 Six Forks Road, Raleigh, North Carolina 27615, 800-334-9270.

• Mortgage Guaranty Insurance Corp, Post Office Box 488, MGIC Plaza, Milwaukie, Wisconsin 53201-0488, 800-558-9900.

• PMI Mortgage Insurance Company, 601 Montgomery Street, San Francisco, California 94111, 800-288-1970.

• Republic Mortgage Insurance Company, Post Office Box 2514, Winston-Salem, North Carolina 27102-9954, 800-999-7642.

• Triad Guaranty Insurance Corp, Post Office Box 2300, Winston-Salem, North Carolina 27102, 800-451-4872.

• United Guaranty Corp, Post Office Box 21567, Greensboro, North Carolina 27420-1367, 800-334-8966.

Publications

- *Buying Your Home: Settlement Costs and Helpful Information.* Mortgage lenders are required to give a copy of this publication to all borrowers at loan application. Contains information to assist borrowers in shopping for services when buying and financing a home. Available free from any mortgage lender.
- *Fannie Mae Consumer Guide to ARMs.* The pros and cons of adjustable rate mortgages and fixed rate mortgages. Available free from Fannie Mae's Consumer Resource Center, 800-732-6643.

Research and statistics on housing

- Washington Center for Real Estate Research (WCRER), Washington State University, Post Office Box 644861, Pullman, Washington 99164-4861, 509-335-7080, 800-835-9683, 509-335-7863, web site, e-mail wcrer@wsu.edu. Collects and disseminates information on real estate markets and the real estate industry throughout Washington, including the Housing Affordability Index which is calculated quarterly for each county in the state.

Index

Adjustable rate mortgage 93, 114-116
Affordable housing 209-210
Age of structure 55-56
Agency
    Buyer agency 25-26, 33-34, 73
    Commissions 30-35, 44-46
    Disclosure 26-27
    Disclosure form (Oregon) 28-29
    Dual agency 26
    Exclusive buyer's agent 30
    Fiduciary obligations 21-22
    Finding an agent 36-41, 212
    Floor time (up time) 40
    Friend in the business 37
    Law of agency (defined) 21-22
    Licensing agencies 47, 211
    Minimum standards 39
    Part-time agents 38
    Seller agency 22-25
    Subagents 24-25
Alternative property tactic 80
American Society of Home Inspectors 211
Amerin Guaranty Corp 215
Amortization 95-96, 205-207
Appraisal 69-71, 79, 132-133
Appreciation 9, 14-17, 49-66
    Age of structure 55-56
    Appreciation vs inflation 49-50
    Curb appeal 53
    Distressed properties 65-66, 70-72
    Location 61-63

Assignment 161-163
Associate broker 19-20
Assumption 119-120
Bankruptcy
    Contract law 148
    Credit qualifying 126
Blind assumption 120
Broker 19
Builders 43
Buydowns 96-100
Buyer agency 25-26, 33-34, 73
Buying vs renting 10-16
Cancellation (contracts) 148
Capital gains 14-15
Caps 93-94
Certificate of eligibility 105
Certified Residential Broker 21
Certified Residential Specialist 21
Chicago Title Insurance 65-66
Choice strategy 81
Clients' trust account 79, 156-157
Close (and pitch) 75
Closing 167-186
Closing date 158
Combination loan 118-119
Commissions 30-35, 175
Commonwealth Mortgage Assurance Co. 215
Comparative Market Analysis (CMA) 70, 79
Conditions 82-83, 152-154
Contingencies 82-83, 152-154
Conventional loans 108, 111-119

Conversion privilege 93
Cost of Funds Index (COFI) 115-116
Counteroffers (contract law) 144-145
Credit repair 127-128
Credit reports 125-130, 210
Credit scoring 128-130
Curb appeal 53
Disclosure
    Forms 187-204
    Seller 148-152
Discounts (loan) 96-100
Distressed properties 65-66, 70-72
Dual agency 26
Due on sale clause 93
Duties of the agent 21-22
Earnest money
    Agreement (contracts) 155-164
    Deposit 78-79, 154-157
Easements 157
Equifax 210
Escrow
    Agents' accounts, for clients' funds 79, 156-157
    Closing transactions 105, 163, 167-186
    Closing instructions 169-172
    Impounds for taxes and insurance 11, 14, 181-182
Exclusive agency listing 44
Exclusive buyer's agent 30
Exclusive right to sell listing 44-45
Experian 210
Extender clause (listings) 44
Fair, Isaac Company 128-130
Fannie Mae 88-89, 111, 213, 216
Federal Agricultural Mortgage Corporation 111
Federal Home Loan Mortgage Corporation 88-89, 111, 213

Federal Housing Administration 87-88, 100-104, 108, 111, 214
Federal Reserve Board 213
Federal Reserve Regulation Z 140
Federal Trade Commission 210
Fiduciary obligations (agents) 21-22
Financial calculator 207-208
Financing 87-122
    Adjustable rate mortgage 93, 114-116
    Amortization 95-96
    Application 124-125
    Appraisal 69, 79, 132-133
    Assumption 119-120
    Buydowns 96-100
    Caps 93-94
    Certificate of eligibility 105
    Combination loan 118-119
    Comparative Market Analysis (CMA) 70, 79
    Conventional loans 108, 111-119
    Conversion privilege 93
    Cost of Funds Index (COFI) 115-116
    Credit repair 127-129
    Credit reports 125-130
    Credit scoring 128-130
    Discounts 96-100
    Due on sale clause 93
    Fair, Isaac Company 128-130
    Fannie Mae 88-89, 111, 213, 216
    Federal Agricultural Mortgage Corporation 111
    Federal Home Loan Mortgage Corporation 88-89, 111, 213
    Federal Housing Administration 87-88, 100-104, 108, 111, 214
    Federal Reserve Board 213
    Funding fee 105

Index

Government National Mortgage Association 88-89, 111, 213
Index 93, 114-116
Loan to value ratio 93
London Interbank Offered Rate (LIBOR) 116
Margin 93, 114-116
Mortgage brokers 91-92
Mortgage credit certificate 110
National Housing Act 87-88
Negative amortization 94
Nehemiah down payment assistance 103-104
No-doc loans 114
Nonconforming loan 94
Oregon Department of Housing and Community Services 108-110, 213-214
Oregon Department of Veterans Affairs 107-108, 110-111, 214
Preapproval vs prequalification 67-68, 123-124
Predatory lenders 135-141
Prepayment penalty 94, 134
Private mortgage insurance 117-118, 119, 215
Qualifying ratios 130-132
Rate lock 94, 137-139
Rural Economic Community Development Corporation 111
Secondary mortgage market 88-89, 111
Seller financing 120-122
Servicing 89-91
State bond programs 108-110, 111
Stated income loans 114
Subprime loan 130, 136-137
Teaser rate 94, 115
U.S. Department of Veterans Affairs 104-107, 110, 168, 214-215
Washington State Housing Finance Commission 108-110, 215
Finding an agent 36-41, 212
Fire insurance 11, 181
Fixer-upper 54-55
Fixture 163
Floor time (up time) 40
For sale by owner 41-42
Foreign Investment in Real Property Tax Act 161
Franchise real estate companies 36
Fraud 148-152
Friend in the business 37
Funding fee 105
GE Capital Mortgage Insurance Group 215
Goals of home buyers 9
Government National Mortgage Association 88-89, 111, 213
Graduate of the Realtor® Institute 21
Home inspection services 211
HouseMaster of America 211
Impossibility of performance 147
Impounds 11, 14
Incompetence 147
Index (adjustable rate mortgages) 93, 114-116
Inspections 83-84, 151-152, 211
Insurable title 157
Kickbacks 174
Latent defect 151
Law of agency 21-22
Lease-options 165-166
Legal description 144
Leverage 17-18
Licensing agencies 47, 211
Lien 163

Listing agreements 44-46
Loan application 124-125
Loan qualifying ratios 130-132
Loan to value ratio 93
Location, location, location 61-63
Loan servicing 89-91
London Interbank Offered Rate (LIBOR) 116
Maintenance expense 11
Margin 93, 114-116
Market value 69-71, 79
Marketable title 157
Material fact (contracts) 150-151
Million Dollar Club 37
Minimum acceptable standards (agent) 39
Misrepresentation 148-152
Mortgage brokers 91-92
Mortgage credit certificate 110
Mortgage Guaranty Insurance Corp 215
Mortgage insurance 117-118, 119, 215
Mortgage interest
   Chart 12
   Income tax deduction 12-14
Multiple listing service 45
Mutual mistake (contracts) 147
National Association of Exclusive Buyers Agents 212
National Association of Realtors® 20-21, 212
   Designations 21
National Housing Act 87-88
Negative amortization 94
Negotiating 72-86
Nehemiah down payment assistance 103-104
Nibbling 83
No-doc loans 114
Nonconforming loan 94

Northwest Multiple Listing Service 155
Obligations of the agent 21-22
Offers (contract law) 144-147
One-party listing 46
Open listing 44-45
Options 164-165
Oregon Association of Realtors® 155
Oregon Department of Housing and Community Services 108-110, 213-214
Oregon Department of Veterans Affairs 107-108, 110-111, 214
Oregon Real Estate Agency 211
Oregon Revised Statutes 211
Part-time agents 38
Pitch (and close) 75
PMI Mortgage Insurance Company 215
Possession date 158
Preapproval vs prequalification 67-68, 123-124
Predatory lenders 135-141
Preliminary title report 157
Prepaid interest 179-181
Prepayment penalty 94, 138, 141
Prime credit (and subprime) 130, 136-137
Principal gain 14, 95-96
Private mortgage insurance 117-118, 119, 215
Property taxes 10-13
Prorate date 158, 171
Rate lock 94, 134-139
Real Estate Buyers Agent Council (NAR) 212
Real Estate Owned (REO) Department 65
Real Estate Settlement Procedures Act 140-141, 158, 173-186, 214

Index

Realtor® 19-20, 47, 212-213
Recording 161, 184-185
Regulation z 140
Renting vs buying 10-16
Republic Mortgage Insurance
   Company 215
Rescission (contracts) 148
Reserves 11, 14, 181-182
Revised Code of Washington 211
Rural Economic Community
   Development Corporation
   111, 214
Safety clause (listings) 44
Sales associate 19
Salesperson 19
Secondary mortgage market 88-89,
   111
Seller agency 22-25
Seller disclosure 187-204
Seller financing 120-122
Servicing (loans) 89-91
Settlement date 158
Shakespeare 9
Specific performance (contracts)
   154-155
Standard form title insurance
   policy 163, 182-184
State bond programs 108-110, 111
Stated income loans 114
Statutory warranty deed 161, 171
Subagents 24-25
Supreme Court (Oregon) 143
Survey 185-186
Teaser rate 94, 115

Time is of the essence 163
Title insurance
   Customer service 42
   Policies 157, 163, 182-184
Trans Union 210
Triad Guaranty Insurance Corp
   215
Trust deed 163
Truth in Lending Act 140
Unenforceable contract 147-154
Uniform Settlement Statement
   140, 174-186
United Guaranty Corp 215
Up time (floor time) 40
U.S. Department of Agriculture
   214
U.S. Department of Housing &
   Urban Development (HUD)
   214
U.S. Department of Veterans
   Affairs 104-107, 110, 214-215
Usury 139-140
Value 69-71, 79
Warranty deed 161, 171
Washington Association of
   Realtors® 155
Washington Center for Real
   Estate Research 216
Washington Real Estate Com-
   mission 211
Washington State Housing
   Finance Commission 108-110,
   215
Wright, Frank Lloyd 53

...YOU'RE ABSOLUTELY RIGHT - SWSDOB MEANS 'SITUATED WITHIN SNIFFING DISTANCE OF BREWERY...'
REALTY GUIDE